The Scots Philosophical Monograph Series

While this monograph series is published on behalf of the Scots Philosophical Club, refereed by a panel of distinguished philosophers in the Club, and has as one of its aims the provision of a publishing outlet for philosophical work being done in Scotland, it is nevertheless international. The Club hopes to bring out original works, written in a lively and readable style, and devoted to central areas of current philosophical concern, from philosophers working anywhere in the world.

As a deliberate policy we have specified no areas of the subject on which the series is to concentrate. The emphasis is on originality rather than, say, on surveys of literature, commentaries on the work of others, or exegesis. Historical works will be included only in so far as they also contribute significantly to topical debates.

As well as our debt to the referees and consulting editors, we have to acknowledge a very real debt to the universities of Glasgow, Edinburgh, Aberdeen, Stirling and St Andrews who—despite the current stringencies—have given financial support to the series.

Series Editors: Andrew Brennan, William Lyons

Consulting Editors:

Professors G H Bird *Stirling*
J R Cameron *Aberdeen*
Robin Downie *Glasgow*
Bernard Mayo *St Andrews*
A G Wernham *Aberdeen*
Crispin Wright *St Andrews*

Scots Philosophical Monographs Number Three

APPROPRIATING HEGEL

Scots Philosophical Monographs

Scots Philosophical Monographs Number Three

APPROPRIATING HEGEL

CRAWFORD ELDER

Series Editors *Andrew Brennan & William Lyons*

ABERDEEN UNIVERSITY PRESS

First published 1980
Aberdeen University Press
A member of the Pergamon Group

British Library Cataloguing in Publication Data
Elder, Crawford
Appropriating Hegel. — (Scots
Philosophical Monographs. 3 ISSN
0144-3062)
1. Hegel, Georg Wilhelm Friedrich
I. Title   II. Brennan, Andrew
III. Lyons, William E   IV. Series
193   B2948

ISBN 0 08 025729 1

PRINTED IN GREAT BRITAIN AT.
ABERDEEN UNIVERSITY PRESS

Contents

Preface

A number of philosophers in recent years have expressed an interest in reexamining Hegel in order to gain new light on various problems in contemporary American and European philosophy.[1] One such problem is the problem of devising a non-dualist philosophy of mind which also will avoid reductivism. This monograph undertakes such a reexamination to just this end. Previous efforts at reexamining Hegel, for the purpose of gaining light on mind-body issues, have fallen short for either of two reasons. On the one hand some such efforts have failed to match the qualifications of a reexamination: a reexamination must bring out new and unnoticed aspects of a philosophy, but several recent returns to Hegel have not found it possible to render his views intelligible except by seeing them as extensions of Kant, Fichte, expressivism, and the like; and hence as, fundamentally, a noticed, familiar, and old philosophy. On the other hand some recent treatments of Hegel's views on mind-body issues have brought forth no positions on issues currently under discussion that are specific enough to engage assent or opposition. This monograph seeks to avoid both of these shortcomings. It sets forth a certain central line of Hegel's thought as independent of Kantian, expressivist, etc. presuppositions, and as being plausible on its own account; and it depicts this line of thought as making a specific contribution to contemporary inquiry on mind and body.

The contribution is this. Recent studies on the relation between mind and body have concentrated upon the concept of mind, and have inquired whether, and in what ways, that concept may be dispensable or replaceable. In particular, it has been asked whether, in an adequate account of human behaviour, psychological principles which appear to explain and to govern human behaviour are reducible to neurophysical laws; or are anomalous from the standpoint of physical sciences; or can, without loss of information, be omitted from an adequate account of human behaviour; or are, for purposes other than prediction, indispensable; etc. What Hegel has to offer to inquiry into the relation between mind and body is, in effect, an approach which focuses on the other side of the nexus. Hegel is, in effect, concerned with the concepts and categories under which we conceive of *material* objects and their behaviour. He seeks to determine the role which *these* concepts occupy in a sound conceptual economy. The position which Hegel advances is that these concepts are, for strictly conceptual reasons, indispensable for any sound conceptual scheme, but also that, in any sound conceptual scheme, use of them is necessarily flanked by use of the concepts of rationality and intentional agency. We must speak of physical objects and physical behaviour, but must also speak—and with equal intended literalness—of minds. Hence there is, on Hegel's position, no question of reducing the concept of mind. At the same time, Hegel's position is different from dualism. It is not, on Hegel's view, the accidental fact that the world contains two Cartesian substances, that explains why concepts of conscious agency get used alongside the concepts of physical objects and behaviour. The connection between these two families of concepts is instead a conceptual one: use of physical concepts *is*, just by its very nature, part of a conceptual practice in which psychological concepts also are used, and *vice versa*; so that we need not commit ourselves to affirming some empirical, or covertly empirical, answer on the question *why* use of either family gets flanked by use of the other. For no other usage is even possible.

A genuinely new approach can therefore be found, in Hegel's philosophy, to problems about mind and body currently under discussion; but this new approach is to be found in Hegel's philosophy of physical objects, rather than in Hegel's social philosophy or philosophy of history. This monograph will consequently have a different focus from most recent work on Hegel. The central location for Hegel's philosophy of physical objects might seem, judging simply by titles, to be *The Philosophy of Nature*; but in fact the positions taken in *The Philosophy of Nature* depend, almost invariably, upon arguments and positions advanced in the *Logic*. This monograph will therefore deal with the *Logic*. Yet it will not deal with the *Logic* as a whole, and will not be a commentary. Numerous discussions in the *Logic* are unsuccessful, overly complicated, or unnecessary for the development of the overall argument. The aim in this monograph will be to concentrate upon a connected and plausible argument, which runs through the length of the *Logic,* and which supports the position on objects and mind just stated. That this argument is the central and dominant message of the *Logic* itself, I believe, but shall not directly argue; indirect evidence to this effect should be provided just by the sheer bulk of those parts of the *Logic* which are, as I will show, involved in the argument which I consider.

Introduction

I. I remarked in the Preface that, for Hegel, the concepts through which we conceive physical objects and their operations can be used soundly only if used in a conceptual scheme which makes use, on an equal footing, of the concepts of mind and of rational agency. The reason why this is so, for Hegel, is that use of the concepts covering physical objects and arrangements requires that we users, wittingly or unwittingly, treat these things as being raw material for purposive employment by rational subjects. Physical objects and arrangements must in effect get conceived as bearing, essentially, a certain general role—the role, that is, of calling forth and giving place for cognitive and practical endeavours by subjects. Now before considering how Hegel could back up such a position, I wish to consider just what this position involves. For in holding that physical objects must in effect be treated as being essentially the bearers of a certain role, Hegel is taking up a *teleological* view of physical objects, in at least one sense of the word. And it may seem that if Hegel holds a teleological view of physical objects, in any sense of the word, then that fact alone must disqualify his views from serious consideration as a contemporary alternative. For is it not, in fact, a fundamental feature of philosophical outlooks from the Enlightenment onwards, that nature is regarded as being not intrinsically teleological? This misgiving is one which requires to be dealt with here at the outset, even at the cost of anticipating some of Hegel's teachings.

There are, as Hegel maintains, different forms of teleology. The teleology which thinkers of the Enlightenment rejected, and which we also regard as absurd, is what Hegel terms 'finite' teleology; the teleology which Hegel himself espouses, Hegel terms 'infinite' teleology.[1] Finite teleology is a concept which claims descent from Aristotle. Employment of it is tantamount to the position that at least some physical occurrences, or at least some physical outcomes, can genuinely be explained by referring to some end or need which thereby is met. It is not necessary that the end or need in question be consciously entertained by some conscious agent, for the end or need is held able to 'act' or 'work' by itself, rather than through the proxy of some conscious intention or desire.[2] The physical occurrence or outcome is said, simply, to have been 'the work of' this or that particular end, or this or that particular end is said to have 'realized itself' in the occurrence or outcome: and this observation is held to be an *adequate* explanation of the occurrence or outcome. It is regarded as unnecessary to mention physical conditions which exist prior to the occurrence or outcome in question and which are sufficient conditions of the occurrence or outcome. In other words, it is thought possible to *explain* the occurrence or outcome while yet treating it, so far as any *physical* account goes, as 'spontaneous'.[3]

Hegel himself joins the Enlightenment thinkers and us in rejecting this 'finite' teleology as absurd: he mentions, as an example of its use, the explanation that cork trees produce their characteristic bark so that there may be stoppers, and goes on to comment, of such explanations, that 'it is easy to see that they promoted the genuine interest neither of religion nor of science'.[4] His own concept of 'infinite' teleology is of a different character. In particular, an object which essentially is the bearer of a role within Hegel's 'infinite' teleology may also be such, essentially, as to behave in a way which is non-spontaneous, 'mechanical', and 'blind'; indeed some role-bearers in infinite teleology *must* behave in such a way. Hence the modern view of physical objects does not remove them from, but rather qualifies them for, the teleology which Hegel espouses.

What then *is* 'infinite' teleology? Hegel indicates that the concept derives from Aristotle's concept of an *energeia,* i.e. of an act whose aim is itself;[5] and it will be easiest to approach the concept by first considering some Aristotelian examples of this Aristotelian original. The activity by which a living creature keeps itself alive is one prime example of an *energeia.* For in providing its various organic needs and ends, a living creature does not work towards being one day rid of organic needs and ends, but rather towards continuing to live—that is, continuing to go on meeting organic needs and ends. A second example of an *energeia* is provided by scientific inquiry, i.e. by what Aristotle calls 'thinking': for in scientific inquiry we pursue one specific question after another, but need not, in so doing, either expect or wish to be rid one day of all questions. We may be as interested in bringing new questions to light as in solving old ones. Our motivation, in pursuing our specific inquiries, may lie simply in the pursuing of specific inquiries, in general. This, then, is the characteristic feature of an *energeia*: that in performing it we function purposively, in various ways, just so as to function purposively, in just such ways as those.

Hegel's 'infinite' teleology is a generalized form of the concept of an *energeia.* The end, in 'infinite' teleology, is not this or that specific end in particular—as is the case with 'finite' teleology—but is rather the enactment, the getting-realized, of specific ends in general. The end, in 'infinite' teleology, is the second-order end of there being purposive work towards ends (in general) (*EL,* § 212). Now for such a process of open purposivity to be carried out, there must evidently be three things. First, there must at any given time be some specific end or ends to be aimed at, some end or ends as yet unrealized; second, there must be agents who do the aiming at, and the work toward, these specific ends; and third, there must be objective materials, in which each specific end is as yet unrealized, but in which and through which each specific end may get realized.

It is in this third dimension that Hegel's concept of 'infinite' teleology overlaps the modern conception of nature as non-spontaneous and mechanical. For consider what features must be had by objects whose role it is to serve as materials on which specific purposive endeavours, in open succession, can be trained. Such objects must, in the first place, be such as to call forth practical work, and hence they must not, in general, be such as spontaneously to conform to particular ends. They must in general conform to ends only to the extent that work is expended upon them; they must conform to ends only accidentally and 'blindly'.[6] At the same time, these objects must be such that work can *make* them conform to specific ends. And they must therefore behave, and alter, in accordance with physical law. For if the eventual conformity to an end were only spontaneous, only a miracle, then no claim could be made out that the conformity was produced *by* the particular work that was expended; we can award success to a given piece of work, only to the extent that the outcome is *its* reflection, according to physical law. It is important, in the second place, to note that the objects which serve as materials for specific endeavours may call forth *cognitive* endeavours as well, and those too in open succession. But here too the roles which objects play within infinite teleology overlap with the modern conception. Only objects whose behaviour is the 'mechanical reflection' of prior conditions can provide *material* for specific scientific questions. And only occurrences which have causes that themselves were caused by prior causes—or which are the reflection of forces themselves brought into play by other forces, etc.—can provide material for cognitive inquiries in open succession.

Hegel's 'teleological' view of physical objects and arrangements is therefore not reactionary or 'unscientific', in the way which the views usually called 'teleological' are. It qualifies—so far as existing criticisms of teleology go—as a candidate for contemporary consideration.

II.   There is, however, one further misgiving about Hegel's view of physical objects which also requires early consideration. I began in the last section by stating that on Hegel's view, physical objects must in effect be conceived as bearing, essentially, the role of raw material for the specific purposive endeavours of subjects. I then showed that this characterization of physical objects was not incompatible with a characterization of them as being, essentially, such as to behave in a non-spontaneous, law-governed, and blind way. But compatibilities run both ways. If objects which essentially are 'mechanistic' also *may* be conceived as role-bearers within infinite teleology, then such role-bearers within infinite teleology also *may* be conceived as 'mechanistic' objects. The remaining misgiving is that it is, despite all that Hegel can say, more natural, or more reasonable, or more cautious to stay with the modern conception of nature as 'mechanistic', than to shift to the compatible Hegelian alternative. How, in other words, can Hegel argue that physical objects *must*—and not only *may*—be conceived as essentially role-bearers?

Now in weighing whether or not Hegel's teleology is uncautious—or whether it is, on the contrary, unavoidable—we must not of course forget that it differs in import from other 'teleological' views of physical objects. It does not amount to a view that physical objects operate spontaneously, possess 'entelechies', are 'ensouled', etc. Just what, however, *does* it amount to? In part, it amounts to the rather abstract (or 'logical') position which I stated before: viz. that the concepts through which physical objects and behaviour are designated can soundly be used only if used in a conceptual scheme in which concepts of rational agency also are used, and are used as equally primitive. Yet this position is, for Hegel, part of a more fundamental and more general one. The reason *why* 'physical' concepts must get used together with 'psychological' ones is, for Hegel, that 'physical' concepts must get used, in effect, as referring to role-players within an organized project of there being ongoing purposive work by subjects: *yet the same also is true of all other concepts. All* concepts and categories, for Hegel, must get used in such a way as to end up representing their referents as role-players within such an organized project. This is true of the concepts through which we designate reasons and excuses, or physical measurements, or psychological influences, or even individual agents themselves. Hegel's teleology is, in other words, not simply a teleology of physical objects, but of everything. And hence the 'logical' position which Hegel's teleology amounts to is actually stronger than the 'logical' position stated thus far. It is the claim that 'physical' concepts must, because *all* concepts must, be used in a conceptual scheme rich enough to depict a project of ongoing purposive activity by subjects—a scheme which, in particular, makes use of the concept of rational agency. A different expression of this same 'logical' position is that there is, in a sense, only *one* concept which soundly can be used at all: for use of any 'particular' concept must amount to a use, stressing one aspect or another, of the overall concept of an organized project of ongoing rational purposivity, which concept Hegel terms 'the idea'.

What follows is that misgivings about the 'reasonableness' or 'cautiousness' of Hegel's teleological views must amount to misgivings about just this 'logical' position. Such misgivings must amount to the tentative conviction that at least some of our concepts can or could be used—so far as any *conceptual* requirements go—within a scheme which made no representation or rational agents, as such, or of their characteristic activities. On such a view, it would be some empirical fact about the world, rather than the intrinsic character of the concepts through which physical objects are designated, which explained why use of these concepts is in fact flanked by use of concepts of rational agency. Now there are, in fact, two large reasons for feeling that the latter view is true, and Hegel's 'logical' position false. First, it seems that we in fact do not use concepts of physical objects in such a way as to treat physical objects as being essentially raw materials for subjective endeavours, and do not draw any other conceptual connections, either, between 'physical objects' and 'conscious agents'. Second, it seems that whatever we may in fact do, what we should do—and can do—is to use concepts of physical objects, of conscious agents, etc., which are conceptually independent of other concepts, and which have a clear and definite sense (or use) in their own right, whatever the context in which they are used. These two objections, then, formulate the misgiving, about a *need* to adopt Hegel's teleological view, in clearer form than before. What answers can Hegel make to them?

Hegel can argue, in answer to the first objection, that we tend to give mistaken reports of the use which we do, and must, make of many of our concepts. He can hold, that is, that we tend to suppose our concepts to have sound and stable use in various contexts where they do not in fact have sound or stable use. Similar contentions, though of more limited scope, are familiar in the philosophy of mind. For it often is argued that we tend— when following common sense—to suppose, mistakenly, that the concepts covering conscious attitudes and sensory experiences have a use independent of the concepts covering overt behaviour, and can or could be used in contexts in which no use is made of these latter concepts. And sometimes, though rather less often, it is also argued that we err when we report that the concepts covering one species of conscious attitude can be used independently of concepts covering other species of conscious attitude: for example, that 'beliefs' can be mentioned quite independently of mentioning 'inclinations' or 'desires', that 'pleasure' and 'pain' can be discussed quite independently of discussing 'preference' and 'aversion', etc. There is of course some tendency, even among philosophers, to suppose that the users of a given concept must, just 'automatically', be able to give accurate general reports of the use which they do and would make of it. Philosophers influenced by this tendency are inclined to react to the rather surprising comments which Hegel makes, concerning the use of concepts covering physical objects and other items, by supposing that Hegel's comments just *obviously* cannot be true of 'our' concepts of physical objects, etc., and must instead be intended as recommendations that we *revise* 'our' concepts; hence such philosophers tend to subscribe to the opinion that Hegel aims at being a 'revisionary metaphysician'. Hegel himself indicates the opposite intention, in such remarks as these: 'When we hear the Idea spoken of, we need not imagine something far away beyond this mortal sphere. The idea is rather what is completely present; and it is found, however confused and degenerated, in every consciousness' (*EL*, second Zusatz to § 213). And, in the *Science of Logic:* 'For this reason too *there is* nothing, whether in *actuality* or in *thought,* that is as simple and as abstract as is commonly imagined. A simple thing of this kind is a mere *presumption* that has its ground solely in the unconsciousness of what is actually present' (*SL,* p. 829).

The second objection to Hegel's 'logical' position is that however we may in fact use our concepts, what we should, and can, do is to give each of our concepts a use independent of others. We should not—and certainly need not—make the use of our concept of 'physical object' meaningful only in contexts where there is actual use, or at least availability, of the concept 'rational agent'. What we should, in general, do, is instead to fix for each of our concepts a coverage or sense which is not altered, distorted, or cancelled even when radical changes should occur in the context of use. For only so—this objection reasons—can the sense which each concept does have be definite and clear. This objection to Hegel's 'logical' position is rather less familar then the first. But that it is at least as worthy of attention emerges if we consider the most basic features of contemporary philosophical method. Contemporary philosophy devotes considerable efforts to determining what are the necessary and sufficient conditions for the application of various important concepts, and pursues such inquiries by considering widely varying contexts of application for these concepts: it is throughout assumed without hesitation that there is, for each 'important' concept, a fixed coverage, invariant despite these variations in contexts. Or consider how we would currently approach even a claim such as Hegel makes, in holding that physical objects, physical laws, conscious agents, and human societies are all essentially role-players in a single project: we would regard it as essential to consider each of these elements in turn, independently of the others, and to see then what sort (if any) of an overall picture could be asserted.

What, then, is Hegel's answer to this second objection? The attitude towards concepts which this objection voices is the attitude which Hegel, using the vocabulary of mental faculties, calls 'the Understanding': and the *Logic* as a whole is framed as a rejection, precisely, of 'the Understanding'. Hegel's rejection is, however, stronger than it logically has to be. Hegel rejects the suggestion that we *must* frame concepts which are separate and independent from one another by showing it false even that we *may* frame concepts which are separate and independent from one another. Hegel's defence against the Understanding coincides, therefore, with his argument for what I have termed his 'logical' position. And since that 'logical' position is what Hegel's teleological view of the world amounts to, Hegel's defence against the Understanding coincides with his argument for his teleological view of the world—and in particular, of physical objects.

III.   I commented, at the start of the preceding section, that the misgiving about there being any real *need* to adopt Hegel's teleological view required early consideration. So it does. It also is useful, before entering into the details of the argument of the *Logic,* to have some general indication of the outlines of that argument. To meet the former need as well as the latter—at least part way—I will close this Introduction with a brief sketch of the *Logic.*

Hegel's general approach in the *Logic* is to give, to the Understanding, rope enough to hang itself. He considers a wide range of concepts and catagories which do, in varying degrees and ways, match the requirements of the Understanding. These are concepts and categories which have been assigned an application that is independent of, and unaffected by, the employment of other concepts and categories. Affinities or connections among concepts, to the extent that these obtain at all, are regarded as being the function, not of the intrinsic assigned sense of each concept, but rather of extrinsic contingencies of the actual employments of concepts. Hence internally, the concepts endorsed by the Understanding are simple: and these two features, viz. internal simplicity and external independence, are characteristic (in varying degrees) of all the concepts criticized in the *Logic.*

The content of Hegel's criticism is, in general, this: that concepts assigned such a context-independent use, and sense, prove on examination to have no sound or stable use at all, and hence no genuine sense. Concepts cannot, in fact, successfully be assigned any use at all other than use together with an overall conceptual scheme which contains the conceptual reasources needed to designate a project of ongoing purposive activity by rational agents, as such. Or, to speak of this overall conceptual scheme as itself a concept, concepts cannot be used at all except as aspects of the Idea. Now this positive contention is sometimes expressed, both by interpreters and by Hegel himself, as the position that the Idea is *the only* sound concept, or that the Idea *alone* 'is the truth', etc.[7] Yet this does not at all mean that concepts such as Quality, Thing, Force, Cognition, etc. have no sound application whatever. They do have application, but they have application only as aspects of the Idea, i.e. only together with the overall conceptual scheme.

The manner in which Hegel makes his criticism of concepts assigned a context-independent use by the Understanding is, as I have said, to give these concepts rope enough to hang themselves. Hegel shows, or seeks to show, that concepts rendered thus independent prove unusable just by themselves, and on internal grounds; no special assumptions are said to be employed in showing them unusable. The potential for collapsing which is shown by the concepts tailored by the Understanding is called, by Hegel, their 'indwelling' dialectic. (The term 'dialectic' is also applied to the philosophical depiction of such a collapse. In no case, however, is the term 'dialectic' used to indicate a *method*, for doing or showing something, describable apart from *what* is shown.[8])

The *Logic*, like all of Hegel's published works, has three parts. In the first part—the Doctrine of Being—Hegel considers what might be called the concepts and categories of surface description, for example the concept of being composed of seven units, or of being red, or of being cold.[9] These concepts and categories are the natural starting-point for Hegel since they appear, even without special stipulations, to be concepts of just that sort which the Understanding recommends that we use. Being red, for example, seems to be a simple determination, free of internal aspects or complexities; it also seems to be an independent and self-standing determination. To say that this item is red is not (it seems) to say or imply anything else about it, nor about any other item. But Hegel argues that such suppositions about the categories of Quantity and Quality are really in conflict with the only *use* which we could profitably make of these categories. For example—to begin with a very simple point—the idea that an item is red will lose all its characteristic punch or content, unless we *apply* this idea in a context in which we are also willing to say that some other item is black or orange, or might be black or orange. That is, the concept of red can have significant use only when it is applied along with the concepts of contrary opposites. Hegel also wants to make a point about the very categories of Quality and Quantity themselves; in fact, this is his *main* point in the first part of the *Logic*. He says we tend to suppose the category or concept of Quality is independent in its sense or coverage from that of Quantity, and vice versa: the idea of Quality is one idea, and the idea of Quantity is quite another idea, distinct from Quality. But Hegel argues that if Quality and Quantity are actually used in a way which bears out this supposition, then they are not used in a significant or stable way at all. The only sound use of these concepts is one which ties them in with one another. The only sound use of Quality is one which *in effect* says to be qualitatively *thus* amounts to *amounting to* some definite quantitative measure; or, in other words, qualities are just what mark out and colour in quantitative determinations. On the other hand, the only sound use of the concept of quantitative measure is one which treats quantitative measure as just a stepping-stone to some qualitative transition. In other words, for a thing to be 200 degrees is for it to be just about to turn into steam, for it to be 70 degrees is for it to be rather far from becoming steam or from undergoing any other qualitative change, etc. Quantity is just the measurer of qualitative flux.

These positions call, however, for the reformulation of the categories of surface description. If the only sound use of the category of Quality is one in which we treat it as the reflection or indicator of something *else*, and if the same is true of the only sound use of the category of Quantity, then either category actually amounts, in use, to a case of the concept-scheme 'reflection-and-underlying ground', or in other words 'manifestation-and-underlying essence'. Hegel therefore turns to the second part of the *Logic*, 'the Doctrine of Essence'. Here Hegel deals with a series of paired concepts, which represent variations on the fundamental scheme of 'manifestation-and-essence', and which might be termed 'the categories of explanation': for example, Force and Expression, Law and Appearance, Substance and Accident. It is characteristic of these paired concepts that one concept in each pair can retain its assigned sense only if used in a context where use is also made of the other concept within that pair; and hence, in the Doctrine of Essence, Hegel deals with concepts which no longer embody, to the fullest degree, the recommendations of the Understanding. A concession is made, in the use of these concepts, that some needed concepts cannot be assigned a use independent of the use of all other, outside concepts. Yet these paired concepts at the same time seem—again without special stipulation—to meet the requirements of the Understanding at least part way. For it seems, in the case of each pair, that *only* one concept depends for its sense upon employment of the other concept. In each pair there seems to be a dominant partner: there seems, that is, to be a concept which *can* have meaningful use even in some contexts where the other is not used at all. And such a dominant concept will permit us to speak, meaningfully, of its referent as obtaining in contexts where no mention is made of the referent of the subordinate concept. Thus it seems meaningful to speak of underlying forces existing, even where no mention is made of concrete expressions which they generate; or to speak of empirical data (Appearances) occurring, even where no mention is made of *any* law that may organize them; etc. But Hegel's contention is that no sound use is possible for concept-pairs which show such one-way dependence as this. Even that concept which, in each case, seems the dominant partner must, in practice, be given a use which depends on a use, in the same context, of what seems the subordinate partner. Actual use of the concept of surface manifestation must end up representing it as being, essentially, only the illustrator-of some underlying principle; but equally, actual use of the concept of an underlying principle must end up representing it, in effect, as being only the underlier-of, the explainer-of, some surface fact.

These positions, however, themselves call for a further reformulation. We earlier saw that, in actual use, the categories of surface description must amount to the concept-scheme 'manifestation-and-underlying-essence'; we now see that this concept-scheme, while it appears to comprise two elements, comprises no elements which can in actual use be separated from one another. It is therefore misleading to represent the pairs of concepts, which are considered in the Doctrine of Essence, as being pairs at all. Such pairs must be reformulated so as to reflect the fact that they function, in use, as single (if complex) concepts. This is the task of the third part of the *Logic*, titled the Doctrine of the Notion. The reformulation which Hegel offers here involves seeing both surface fact and underlying principle as being essentially role-players in a single, complex job or function. This job is initially characterized as the working of explanatory principles, or, to use a wording closer to Hegel's own terminology, as the dominating of instantial data by the universal (or by 'the notion', and hence the title of this third part). But ultimately, as Hegel argues, this job must be viewed as the occurrence and provision of suitable raw materials for cognitive and practical endeavours by subjects. It must, in fact, be characterized as the Idea.

1

The Doctrine of Being

I. Hegel's chief aim in the Doctrine of Being is, as I have said, to establish a very unusual claim about the 'descriptive' categories of Quality and Quantity: namely, that the only sound or stable use of either category is one which treats that category as being in some way a reflection or function of the other. That is, the only sound application of the concept of being-qualitatively-*thus* is one which says, in effect, 'to be qualitatively thus amounts to amounting to one certain quantitative measure out of a range of quantitative measures'. And the only sound application of the concept of being quantitatively-thus-great or thus-small is one which says, in effect, 'to be thus great amounts to being just on the verge of a certain qualitative transformation, or else to being quite far from some other qualitative transformation. Quantities and quanta then turn out to be just gradings of, references to, qualitative shifts; on the other hand qualities are just reflections of quantitative determinations.

Yet Hegel begins the Doctrine of Being by commenting on a different group of categories altogether. These categories appear, again without special stipulation, to match the recommendations of the Understanding to an even greater degree than do the categories of Quality and Quantity: they are internally simple in the utmost degree, and their application depends not at all on the application of any other concept whatsoever. They are, in fact, such extreme cases of the features which the Understanding urges that they should be regarded as the 'lunatic fringe' of the Understanding's recommendations. But the examination of them is to some extent instructive.

The first of these initial categories is the concept of pure, undifferentiated Being, as in the philosophy of Parmenides. This concept is simply the idea of a wholly blank presence: it is therefore as internally simple as any concept could conceivably be. And since the only use of which the concept permits are assertions of the form 'Being is', use of the concept is quite independent of the use of any other (*EL, §* 86 and *Zusatz*). Yet, as Hegel points out, the concept proves on examination to have actually no sound use at all. Assertions that Being is—that something utterly without content obtains—actually assert nothing at all. In effect, then, the concept of Being just is the concept of a pure Nothing (*EL, §* 87). Or rather pure Being *would* be pure Nothing, if it were not a further feature of our use of Being that we contrast it with Nothing, and claim it is wholly different from Nothing. (Parmenides himself, we may note, expressed himself thus: 'Being *alone* is, *and nothing* is not.') The fact that we draw such a contrast is no casual accident. By drawing such a contrast we make it seem that the assertion of Being is the denial of something else, and that the assertion therefore has some content, amounts to a claim of some sort.[1]

In similar fashion we treat the concept of Nothing as what excludes or contrasts with Being. It follows then that we inevitably use the concepts of Being and Nothing in alternation with one another, treating each as the replacer or supplanter of the other.[2] Our usage here can really be described as the application of a single concept, i.e. the concept of pure Transition or Becoming, in which 'Being' and 'Nothing' figure as opposed but connected 'moments'.[3]

But our use of this concept of Becoming cannot actually be meaningful unless it involves more than we have indicated so far. To speak of Being excluding Nothing which excludes Being, etc., will be to employ an empty alternation of mere *names* unless we can give Being a substantive difference from its opponent. In other words, we can meaningfully use the idea of Transition only where we have two end-points which are themselves genuinely distinguished. But so far Being and Nothing are only *meant, intended,* to differ from one another (*EL, §* 88).

Now we earlier pictured Being as wholly simple, pure, featureless: and there are no contrasts with, or distinctions from, and element like *this*. It is evident, then, that to the extent that Being is soundly applied, Being is treated as Being-thus or Being-so, i.e. as determinate Being, Being-this-way-and-not-that. When we apply the idea of Being-this-way-and-not-that in an assertion we do genuinely *exclude* something—we say 'not that'—and we do provide the logical room for genuine alternation (*EL,* §§ 89-90). But let us note that every form of Being-this-way or Being-thus will have a contrast term which has a definite character of its own.[4] This was not so with Being and Nothing: we in effect *defined* each of these to be different from the other, but provided no distinctive content for each to 'back-up' or 'flesh-out' this difference. We would make a similar error if we said that the contrast-term to Being-thus were just 'Being-not-thus'; for example, that the contrast-term to Being-red were just 'Being-non-red'. In this case the contrast between Being-just-thus and its opponent, or the exclusion of the opponent by Being-just-*thus*, would again be an empty and merely difinitional matter. We would have a positive being which would be distinctive just in that it contrasted with something itself not otherwise specifiable than as 'that which contrasts with the positive Being'. But a contrast with the latter would be an empty contrast.

II.   Hegel therefore turns now to consider more closely the category of determinate Being. The preliminary skirmish with the Understanding is over; Hegel is now dealing, under a different title, with the first of his chief topics in the Doctrine of Being, viz. Quality. In the discussion which now occurs, Hegel employs two terms in unusual senses, and it is easiest simply to follow this usage in commenting upon the discussion. The bearer of a certain determinate Being, a certain distinctive thusness, Hegel calls a 'Something' (*Etwas*); the distinctive thusness which it bears, Hegel calls its 'quality' (*EL,* § 90). These terms are introduced as grammatical conveniences, rather than as ways of smuggling in a substantive new concept. For we are, of course, accustomed to speaking of qualities had (by something), and of items *which* have them; yet Hegel makes plain that he does not here intend to introduce the full-fledged concept of a substance, i.e. of an item which can remain itself while yet acquiring new qualities and losing old ones. The 'bearers' of qualities which Hegel intends here to discuss are, so to speak, just noun-forms of those qualities themselves. As Hegel puts it, 'A Something is what it is in virtue of its quality, and losing its quality it ceases to be what it is'.[5]

Hegel begins his discussion of determinate Being by considering one untenable view of this category which the Understanding tempts us to take. We are tempted to suppose that the idea of Being-specifically-thus involves two separate aspects, an inner and an outer. Internally, that is, it involves the simple possession of a positive quality; externally, it involves the contrasting with some specific other. In other words we tend to take the idea of 'Being-this-way-and-not-that' and to split it up into 'Being-this-way' *and* 'Being-not-that'. These two aspects are called by Hegel 'Being-by-self', and 'Being-for-Another' (*EL,* § 91). But what Hegel argues is that these two aspects are not separate at all, if we look to the only sound use of the concept of determinate Being. For suppose we did treat the characteristic quality of a particular Something as a strictly *intrinsic* feature of that Something, as a feature which had a definite status entirely *apart from* all contrast with any opposite. Then when we applied the idea of this inner character we would exclude nothing, deny nothing: we would be saying 'this item is specifically *thus,* but by that remark alone I don't mean to imply that it is distinctive or different from anything'. Clearly we would in effect be back at the category of bare *Being*. The element which stands in no contrasts to anything is the featureless element, Being.

So Hegel's first conclusion is that Being-for-Another is no external or extrinsic fact about the specific Something; on the contrary, what it is to be specifically thus is to be contrasted with, to be the negation of, some other Something. This means that we can meaningfully use the concept of Something-specifically-thus only where we draw a contrast between this Something and some other Something.[6]

But the contrast we draw will be an empty one, a merely 'intended' contrast, unless we treat the 'other' Something as being itself specific and distinctive. (For our original Something to stand in specific contrast with 'nothing-in-particular', would be for it to stand in no specific contrasts at all.) Yet the only way to treat this other Something as itself being possessed of a definite and distinctive character, is to draw a contrast between it and yet a further Something. Hence meaningful use of the concept of any one specific Something requires specifiability, not just of one or a few 'opponents'—'opponents' which provide opposition to the given Something—but of 'opponents' forming *an endless series*—in which each 'opponent' provides opposition to the Something which goes before. (This point is expressed by Hegel under the image of an 'infinite progression'. The concept of a given qualitative Something can meaningfully be used only where logical room can get specified for an endless series of qualitative alterations; or, as Hegel very misleadingly puts it, one qualitative Something becomes another, which becomes another, etc.[7]) The question which this observation raises is just how it is possible that successive qualitative 'opponents' should be, in this way, specifiable *ad infinitum*. The answer is that what particular qualitative Something comes next in such a series always is, at any point, predictable or computable. What comes next in such a series always is, in a sense, a further case of what has already gone before: what comes next is always just a further embodiment of qualitative opposition or contrast. It is, in other words, because we operate not only with the concept of this particular quality and of that particular quality, but also with the concept of a *universal* common to all these particular qualities, and embodied in each, that this series is for us specifiable *ad infinitum*. And hence it is just because we operate with the concept of such a universal, that concepts of particular qualitative Somethings can have for us meaningful use. This universal of particular Somethings might be labelled 'the qualitatively distinctive in general', or 'the distinctively specific', but Hegel terms it 'Being-for-Self'. And it is this Being-for-Self which now forms Hegel's new topic.[8]

III.   Hegel explains this transition to Being-for-Self by saying that we arrive at Being-for-Self once we abandon the concept of an indefinitely extending series of specific Somethings or Qualities; and that the reason why we are to abandon the latter concept is that it involves the wrong infinity (*EL,* §§ 94-95). Does this mean, then, that we are to regard Being-for-Self as also being somehow 'infinite', but in a 'genuine' or 'good' way? Not really. What Hegel calls a 'wrong' or 'bad' infinite is really precisely what most people mean by 'infinite'. Being-for-Self, if infinite, is infinite only in a very *un*familiar sense peculiar to Hegel. Nonetheless it is worthwhile to consider just what 'infinite' does mean for Hegel. It means 'not delimited by an alien outside other'.[9] Why is Being-for-Self 'infinite' in this sense? For this, we must begin by turning back to the qualitative Something. Each Something is set off by, contrasted with, some outside other Something; each is finite. And even if we say that such contrast with another is *intrinsic* to each Something—even if we say that Being-red just is the contrasting with green—still the other term to the contrast lies, conceptually, outside the original something (greenness is in turn the contrasting with brownness, etc.). But with Being-for-Self the situation is different. Being-for-Self is the general concept of the distinctively specific. And that 'the distinctively specific' always is set off by some contrasting other, is no *extrinsic* fact about the distinctively specific, but is part and parcel of its own intrinsic sense. Being-for-Self is not limited by its opposing other, but is on the contrary realized, made itself, by its opposing other (*EL,* §§ 95-96).

The transition to Being-for-Self does, indeed, require explanation in one further respect as well. The regress through an infinite series of qualitative Somethings, each mentioned individually, is evidently something conceptually inescapable, given a limited conceptual scheme which does not include Being-for-Self itself. Yet Hegel actually depicts this regress as being, not a conceptual regress, but a temporal progression. Each determinate Something is said, as indicated above, to 'become' a different determinate Something (*EL,* § 93). Now it seems clear that this temporal process is only a loose metaphor for a conceptual regress: for one thing, any such process would actually violate the very definition of the 'Something', which cannot, precisely, alter and yet remain in existence at all. We will in fact see that Hegel not infrequently uses the language of physical alteration to express conceptual entailments.

This latest transition, whatever its peculiarities, leaves Hegel at the concept of Being-for-Self: and Hegel turns now to examine this concept more closely. Here Hegel maintains, puzzlingly enough, that Being-for-Self is a unitary One which repels itself from itself into a Many (*EL,* § 97 and *Zusatz*), and then adds that this Many is really an empty plurality which collapses back into a One (*EL*, § 98); and these occurrences are then said to provide us with a transition to the category of Quantity (*EL*, § 98 and *Zusatz*). The sense of these rather oracular remarks is, it would seem, that qualities conceived as instances of Being-for-Self are thereby credited, in effect, with certain *formal* features possessed more noticeably by numerical units. These features, then, we must now consider more closely.

Let us first deal with the so-called 'self-repulsion' of Being-for-Self into a Many. Here Hegel once again uses physical imagery to indicate a conceptual implication. Suppose that the concept of Being-for-Self does have application, suppose that there is at least one instance of it: then it follows immediately that there is *more* than one instance, more than one 'parcel', of Being-for-Self. For Being-for-Self is the concept of the distinctively specific, i.e. of the specifically contrasting. And if we do speak of one actual entity which *is* distinctive, or contrasting, we must necessarily recognize another entity with which it contrasts, and hence an entity which will itself be a second case of 'the distinctively specific', i.e. of Being-for-Self. (This discussion is, though interesting, unnecessary here. Being-for-Self was introduced as a general variable which logically generates or underlies all the various quantitative Somethings. Hence we have known from the start that there would be many different cases of Being-for-Self.)

Hegel next moves on to the claim that this Many, generated by 'self-repulsion' of Being-for-Self, also collapses back into One, which in turn gives us the category of Quantity. These remarks call for a good deal of deentity; but the task need not be difficult, provide we begin by first making a few simple comparisons between Being-for-Self and other, more familiar universals. Being-for-self is itself a universal, of course, just because it has more than one instance (cf. 'self-repulsion'), and because, in particular, the various qualitative Somethings are instances of it. That is, redness is one case or instance of 'the distinctively specific', brownness is another case of 'the distinctively specific', coldness is a third case of distinctive specificity, etc. Let us, now, consider two other universals. Let us take two universals from the pages of Plato and Aristotle: Animality and Number (or 'the Great and Small'). Animality can be said to be instantiated in various individual, concrete entities, but it also can be said to be instantiated, as Aristotle commented, in various specific natures: birdhood, for example, is one specific form or version of Animality, humanness is another, and doghood is a third. Number, also, is embodied or instantiated in various more specific universals: in five-fold-ness (i.e. 5), in seventeen-fold-ness (i.e. 17), etc. Thus far, of course, there is a parallel between these Greek universals and Being-for-Self. For the particular cases of Being-for-Self which have been mentioned—redness, coldness, etc.—could all themselves be regarded as universals.

Yet the parallel with an Animality and Number cannot be complete, since those universals themselves differ from one another in an important respect. In the case of Animality, it is possible to discuss or explain the differences between different specific forms of it. Thus it can be said that humanness is a form of Animality which involves the possession of rationality, whereas birdhood is a form which does not involve rationality and does involve the possession of wings, etc. We can, in other words, state *differentiae* which qualitatively differentiate the different cases of Animality. In the case of Number, however, this is not possible. Five-fold-ness is a different case of Number from eight-fold-ness, but if we attempt to say what *there is* to five-fold-ness that *grounds* its difference from eight-fold-ness, or explains that difference, we find there is nothing to say. Five-fold-ness is of course 'smaller' than eight-fold-ness: but since particular cases of Number can differ from one another only by being smaller than or greater than one another, this comment about five-fold-ness amounts only to a reassertion *that* five-fold-ness is different from eight-fold-ness, and does not provide an explanation *why* five-fold-ness is different from eight-fold-ness. The question *why* five-fold-ness is different from eight-fold-ness is, in fact, an ill-formed question. We could not give, and hence do not ask for, explanations or discussions of the difference between different cases of Number. We differentiate different cases of number not qualitatively, not by mention of *differentiae,* but rather through a kind of conceptual pointing.

Which of these universals is Being-for-Self like? There are a number of different particular cases of Being-for-Self, i.e. of distinctive specificity: there is redness, brownness, coldness, etc. Can we say what there is to the first of these cases of distinctive specificity which renders it a different case of distinctive specificity from the second or third? Can we say that redness is distinctively specific in a different *way* from the way in which brownness is distinctively specific, or coldness, etc.? The answer would seem to be 'No'. Here we are not, as in the case of Animality, mentioning 'different cases' which may be said, in explanation, to *have* different qualities ('differentiae'): we are mentioning 'different cases' which *are*, or which supposedly are, different qualities. All qualitative distinctions belong, in other words, in the category of '*explananda*' if we really set about to *explain* or *discuss* the differences between different cases of Being-for-Self; and hence none can be used to provide *explanantia*.

What follows, then, is that questions *why* different cases of Being-for-Self do differ from one another are really ill-formed, just as are parallel questions about different cases of Number. Different cases of Being-for-Self are distinguished only by a kind of conceptual pointing. And having seen this, we now are in a position to decipher Hegel's remaining two remarks about Being-for-Self. In differentiating different particular cases of Being-for-Self from one another, we draw distinctions which have no specifiable ground, but are instead stipulative or definitional: one case of Being-for-Self differs from another only in that the first is 'just *this* case of Being-for-Self'. But so, of course, is the second. Thus the very act of distinguishing parcels of Being-for-Self, from one another, ends up assimilating them one to another. As Hegel puts it, 'But the Many are the same as one another: each is One, or even one of the Many; they are consequently one and the same. Or when we study all that *Repulsion* involves, we see that as a negative attitude of many Ones to one another, it is just as essentially a connective reference of them to each other; . . .The repulsion therefore has an equal right to be called *Attraction;* and the exclusive One, or Being-for-Self, suppresses itself' (*EL,* § 98). (A corollary of these same observations, which Hegel does not himself point out, is that there is good reason behind our common intuition that alternative dissections of a given quality-space can be equally legitimate. It makes no difference, for example, whether we discern ten different colours in the colour-spectrum, or twelve: for, just because the differentiation of different 'distinctive specificities' is only stipulative, there is no single 'fact of the matter' on the number of colours.)

Hegel also maintains, as indicated above, that the 'repulsion' and 'attraction' of Being-for-Self brings the category of Quantity into our study (*EL,* § 98); and we now are in position to decipher this final remark as well. In discerning a number of different cases of Being-for-Self, of 'the distinctively specific', we discern cases which differ not in *explainable* or qualitative ways from one another, but only in that one case is '*this* case' and another case is '*that* case'. In doing so, we make use of the concept of a set of items which are numerically different from one another, and which, so far as our treatment of them goes, are *only* numerically different. We make use, that is, of a concept more *noticeably* instantiated by sets of *numerical* units, so conceived. For numerical units, even more obviously, are items differentiated from one another not in a qualitative or explicable way, but instead through stipulation.

IV.   Hegel therefore turns now to examine, more closely, the concept or category of Quantity. His ultimate aim is to show that meaningful use of this category requires that users treat particular quantities as measurers of particular qualities. Initially, however, Hegel recognizes that he must assure the reader that the concept or the category which he has just brought forth *is,* in fact, what we ordinarily mean by 'Quantity'.

Hegel's strategy here is to point out that his formulation of the concept of Quantity entails and explains a central feature of the ordinary concept of Quantity: namely, that particular quantities can be regarded either as continuous or as discrete. On Hegel's formulation, the concept of Quantity is the idea of a plurality of items which are numerically distinct from one another, but whose distinctness from one another is not 'backed up' by any differences in character or composition. It is the idea, in other words, of a set of blank units, each distinct from the others, but each having no feature but its distinctness from the others. Now it is easy to see, as Hegel points out, that units so conceived must possess at the same time an aspect of discreteness, *and* an aspect of continuousness (*EL,* § 100 *Zusatz*). Each unit in such a set is regarded as being a genuine item in its own right, something discrete from other units and unitary in itself. On the other hand each unit can be its own distinctive self only by figuring as one unit *among others*: each unit must be contextually connected with others which are indistinguishable from it. Hence the discreteness of each unit is a merely stipulative discreteness: there always is the possibility of changing the boundaries between units, of joining one unit together with its indistinguishable neighbour into a single larger unit, or alternatively of dividing a given unit into several smaller units. In either case, we end up with units which are just as genuinely unitary, and just as genuinely separate, as the original ones.

These points about the *units* in Quantity are coupled, by Hegel, with some points about the particular numbers or 'quanta' by which sets of such units are summed together (*EL,* § 101); and it is with the latter points that Hegel's discussion of Quantity now gets under way. If the units in any given set must, in principle, permit both division into more units and amalgamation into fewer, it follows that the number which expresses the sum of any given set must, in principle, be exchangeable with other numbers both greater and lesser. What we regard as being 12 units can equally well be regarded as being 36, or even 17: there is no one 'fact of the matter'. Or, as Hegel puts it, 'in quantity we have an alterable, which in spite of alterations remains the same'.[10]

These simple observations may seem, however, to raise a question: namely, how can the concepts of specific quanta have any genuine use at all? If, that is, a comment that there are 12 units is exchangeable with the comment that there are *not* 12 units, but 36, what force could either comment have? The answer to this question is, of course, that the concept of any specific quantum is used to indicate a *relation* between some one amount or collection and others, rather than any fact which holds good of that one amount or collection 'by itself'. To say that a given amount measures 12 is to say that that amount is, or would be, greater than any amount which measures 11, when counted in the same units; greater still than any amount which measures 10; etc. It does not matter that the units, by which the given 12 is counted up *as* 12, are distinguished from one another only by stipulation, and hence that the given 12 could also be counted up as a 6, etc. For whatever changes might be made in the way the given 12 is divided up into units and counted, that 12 would still be greater than the set we now count as 11, provided that the same changes were made in the way we divide up and count the units of that 11.

The concepts of specific quanta do have a use, then, just because their use is that of indicating contrasts between one or another given amount and other amounts—indeed, indefinitely many other amounts. Hence, as Hegel says, 'the very notion of quantum is thus to push out and beyond itself' (*EL,* § 104). That is, meaningful use of the concept of any one specific quantum implies, and requires, the wielding of concepts of other, contrasting quanta, without limit (*EL,* § 104).

Yet closer reflection reveals an obscurity concerning the terms between which these contrasts, these relations of 'greater than' and 'less than', get indicated. An amount counted as 12 is made up, as we have seen, of units whose distinctness from one another is only stipulative, and hence any such amount can, as we have seen, be regarded with equal justice as being a 24, a 6, a 17, etc. What follows is that any given 12 must be regarded both as *contrasting* with at least one 24, and also as itself *being* at least one 24. And so, generally, with all instances of all quanta. (As Hegel puts it, when we recollect that a 12 is equally a 24 of units ½ as big, i.e. a 24/2, we see that 12 is both an amount different from and independent of 24, and also something exchangeable, with 'indifference', *with* 24. *EL,* §§ 105-106.)

This obscurity need not, however, amount to an inconsistency of any sort, provided we can draw one crucial distinction. We must be able to say that the 24 with which our give 12 is identical is, in some sense, a different 24 from that 24, or those 24s, with which our given 12 contrasts. We must, that is, be able to maintain that the difference between our 12 and the former 24 is only conventional, only a matter of the way in which 'the same thing' gets counted up, whereas the difference between our 12 and the latter 24 (or 24s) is more than this. To put it still differently, we must be able to maintain that replacement of our 12 with the former 24 makes no real difference, whereas replacement of our 12 with the latter 24 (or 24s) *does* make a real difference. Now this distinction can be drawn, on Hegel's view, just because the difference between two different quanta—e.g. 12 and 24—is such as, in any given case, either to be accompanied by, or to fail to be accompanied by, some other, more substantive, difference. The distinctness between two distinct quanta, that is, can either mark out some *qualitative* difference, or fail to mark out any qualitative difference at all, thereby making no difference. What is essential here is that quantitative differences must be such by nature as to have, in at least some instances, qualitative import. For only so is there the material to draw a distinction between a replacement of 12 by 24 which makes no difference, and one which does make a difference. The concepts of quanta can soundly be used, then, only provided that quanta are treated as being, in at least some contexts, the measurers and graders of qualities. Qualities therefore reappear, at this point, in Hegel's discussion. They now serve to stake out, to give substance to, differences between different points on quantitative continua. Hence a two-way connection—of qualities with quantities, and of quantities with qualities—has now become apparent. We in effect are dealing with the concept of a 'qualitative quantum', or what Hegel calls Measure (*EL*, §§ 107-108).

V.   Two notes should be appended here to Hegel's present position. The first concerns the category of Quality: it can be argued that with the introduction of the category of Measure, Hegel has indicated, not only the necessary setting for sound use of the concepts of specific *quanta,* but also the necessary setting for sound use of the concepts of specific *qualities.* To see this, consider the points which Hegel earlier made concerning specific qualities. Hegel argued, as we saw, that the concept of a specific quality is the concept of an instance of Being-for-Self. And from this it follows, as we noted, that distinctions recognized between different specific qualities are not explicable or grounded, but are stipulative or definitional. If so, however, distinctions recognized between different particular qualities are, in principle, revisable distinctions. If, that is, it is by stipulation that a given range of qualitative content is broken up into specific different qualities, that same range of qualitative content could equally be broken up into an alternative set of specific different qualities. Hence the requirement that particular qualities be regardable as instances of Being-for-Self is in effect a requirement that particular sets of mutually-opposing qualities be regardable as replaceable by different sets. Yet consider, now, what this concept of difference involves. A different set of mutually-opposing qualities could not differ *qualitatively* from that set which it replaces since it would, precisely, be redivision of just the same qualitative content as is systematized by the set that gets replaced. A different set must therefore differ in *form,* rather than in *content*: it must differ from the set it replaces in involving *more* qualities or *fewer*. Hence this concept of difference is the concept of a quantitative difference. And if any given set of qualities must be regardable as replaceable by such a different set, use of the category of Quality requires use of the category of Quantity.

The second note is that Hegel's arguments above on Quantity do not show that for each distinct quantum we necessarily recognize one, and only one, distinct qualitative determination: instead they show that in some central contexts of use, for each specific quantum, we treat that quantum as being such as to have some qualitative import or other. The distinctness of a 200 from a 170 is meaningful as the difference between heavy and light, or as the difference between scorching and hot, or as another qualitative difference. And even within such contexts, we need not exactly assign a distinct quality, in order to provide distinctive qualitative import for a distinct quantum: it suffices to assign a qualitatively distinct shade or degree of some recognized quality. A 200 can differ from a 170 by signifying a yet *hotter* state, even if it does not signify a gaseous, as opposed to a liquid, state.

Supported by these reflections, let us turn now Hegel's own discussion of the qualitative quantum, Measure. The first of the reflections above suggests that Hegel already can conclude, not only that use of the category of Quantity requires use of the category of Quality, but also, conversely, that use of the category of Quality requires use of the category of Quantity. Hegel himself, however, now offers a separate treatment of the latter dependence. This treatment centres on the idea of qualitative *alteration* (*EL,* §§ 108-109). We have ourselves just reviewed the point that since qualities are cases of Being-for-Self, the differences between different particular qualities are stipulative, and that a given quality-space can equally be re-divided, with equal correctness, into more qualities or fewer. The same observation shows that any given qualitative *alteration* can, with equal justice, be construed as an alteration through many different qualities, or instead through only several different qualities, or instead through only a few. Now to the extent that we specify fewer different qualities, to that extent there will be more stages in the alterations that can occur, for which no separate quality-name is available. To that extent, therefore, there will be more alterations which must be regarded as being only quantitative. To the extent that we specify *more* qualities, to that extent there will be more stages in alterations, for which some separate quality-name is available; and in this case a stage quantitatively different from an earlier one will, in more and more cases, also be recognized as involving the advent of a new *quality*. What is fixed in this conceptual picture is simply that some alterations merely quantitative, and some alterations in which a quantitative shift is tied to a marked qualitative change, must necessarily be recognized in the actual use of Quality and Quantity (*EL*, §§ 108-109). In actual use, then, Quality and Quantity must get represented as falling on what Hegel calls the 'nodal line of Measure'. 'This process of measure, which appears alternatively as a mere change in quantity, and then as a sudden revulsion of quantity into quality, may be envisaged under the figure of a nodal (knotted) line' (*EL, Zusatz* to § 109).

Hegel thus arrives at the fundamental conclusion of the Doctrine of Being. The category of Quantity can soundly be used only to the extent that specific quanta get treated as being, by nature, measurers *of* qualitative determinations; the category of Quality can soundly be used only to the extent that specific qualities get treated as being, by nature, reflections of quantitative determinations on quantitative continua (*EL*, § 111). In use, either category must get treated as a reflection or function of the other. In use, therefore, either category in effect amounts to a specific form of the general concept-scheme, 'reflection-and-underlying-ground', or 'manifestation-and-underlying-essence'.

2

The Doctrine of Essence

I. Hegel in the Doctrine of Essence has a two-fold motivation: he wishes to continue the present attack on the Understanding, and he wishes to start some new attacks. The present attack began once the Understanding had recommended the use of what we have called the 'categories of surface description', or what might also be called the 'categories of brute fact'. Hegel has so far argued that if we consider the only sound or stable *use* that could be made of each of these categories of surface description, we will see that each of these categories in effect amounts to a category of surface *reflection*; the categories of brute fact each amount to a category of grounded fact. But Hegel will now go on to argue that the Understanding still has not conceded enough here. The Understanding still seeks to draw clear-cut distinctions between underlying essences and grounded surface manifestations, and to give to either element an independent sense or status of its own. Even these conceptual separations, Hegel will show, are really unworkable; concept-schemes that embody such separation just cannot be used.

Hegel also is interested in launching some new attacks on the Understanding. These new attacks are called forth by new recommendations by the Understanding. The Understanding not only recommends that we use the categories of Being, though those categories meet the criteria of the Understanding very well; the Understanding also recommends that we use various pairs of concepts, in which, in different ways, one element underlies and explains an observable element but is still independent of that observable element, or else, in reverse fashion, one element reflects and illustrates some deep-lying principle but is still independent of that principle. All these concept-pairs fit under the general idea of 'reflection-and-underlying-essence', and so are discussed here in the Doctrine of Essence. But the discussion of them is more or less an extra addition; if Hegel had only wanted to continue his earlier attack, he would not have had to discuss quite a few of these concept-pairs. Hence it is frequently unprofitable to ask how the argument of the Doctrine of Being compels Hegel to consider each concept-pair which appears in the Doctrine of Essence. For frequently, it does not.

Thus, then, Hegel's concerns in the Doctrine of Essence; I wish now to add a brief sketch of the lines along which Hegel will pursue these concerns. Hegel's topic will, as indicated, be various pairs of concepts which are different versions of the general concept-scheme 'surface-manifestation-and-underlying-essence'. Here are a few such pairs, though some on this list are not considered by Hegel:

> Sensory Appearances and Physical Thing
> Processes undergone and enduring Substance
> Expressions and [physical] Force
> Specific empirical Predictions and Scientific Law

Hegel will wish to criticize, not these concept-pairs themselves, but a certain interpretation of such pairs which the Understanding characteristically offers. The Understanding characteristically seeks to represent either depth-element or surface-element as having a kind of conceptual fixity, a definite sense independent of other elements in the conceptual picture, a being or content 'on its own'. The Understanding seeks to give either an A-type or a B-type interpretation to such pairs of concepts:

	A		B
surface-element	Is essentially the reflection of the depth-element	surface-element	Has a being of its own but is also the reflection of the depth-element
depth-element	Has a being of its own but is also the ground of the surface-element	depth-element	Is essentially the ground or explainer or organiser of the surface-element

Thus, to take one of the pairs in the list above, the Understanding tends to give an A-type interpretation to Sensory Appearances and Physical Thing. We tend to feel, that is, that the various sensory appearances which some physical object presents—for example, the various visual looks of a table, the tactile feels of it, even (imaginably) the smell of it—cannot be singled out or discussed at all unless we treat them as appearances of that physical object, appearances produced by that physical object. To the physical object, in contrast, we tend to attribute a being in its own right. That is, we tend to suppose that a given physical object could perfectly well be itself and yet serve as ground to no sensory appearances; for we feel that even if there were no perceivers in the world whatever, and hence no sensory appearances, still this table could perfectly well still 'be there', and be itself. Or, let us take the pair Expressions and Force. Believers in the occult tend to feel that there are certain deep forces which govern various events in the world, but which would still somehow remain at least partly beyond our grasp even if we somehow were to see all their overt expressions. Here too a depth-element is taken to have a standing in its own right, apart from what surface manifestations it may happen to support. Persons of a more scientific cast of mind tend to give a B-type interpretation to Expressions and Force: they hold that there is nothing to a force beyond the sum of the overt expressions it produces, and they may even hold some version of the sophisticated position that a force is just a symbolic fiction which serves to unify scattered but similar phenomena. The expressions, on the other hand, they will regard as identifiable and discussable without reference to any underlying force; these expressions are characterized essentially by a plain descriptive make-up or content. Familiar philosophical arguments can also lead us to give a B-type interpretation to Sensory Appearances and Thing. It can be asked just what we mean by a 'physical thing' which lies *behind* all sensible, knowable, appearances; leading to the phenomenalist position that things are only linguistically-fabricated sets of sensory appearances, which sensory appearances are, for their part, quite self-standing and indifferent to what organization we may linguistically impose on them.

Hegel will argue that both the A-interpretation and the B-interpretation are untenable for pairs which embody the concept-scheme 'manifestation-and-underlying-essence'.[1] He will consider what things would be like if an A-interpretation were accurate, what if a B-interpretation were accurate, and will show, in various specific cases, that either way we would have a pair of concepts which were unusable. The conceptual failures he will narrate characteristically elicit wrong conclusions from the Understanding. The Understanding, on noting that an A-type interpretation cannot be right, characteristically concludes that the corresponding B-type interpretation must be correct; and vice versa. (Consider the reversals that have occurred in the history of philosophy on just the pairs of concepts listed above.) A more reasonable reaction, Hegel feels, would be to decide that conceptual fixity can be assigned neither to surface-element nor to depth-element, giving us what might be called an AB-type interpretation:

AB

Surface-element   Is essentially the reflection of the depth-element
depth-element   Is essentially the ground or explainer or organizer of
                 the surface-element

Yet once we come this far we will also have to go further, for evidently
we have still not given a clear account of a conceptual scheme that will be
workable.[2] We still are suggesting that the concepts which are under consideration are to be regarded as pairs; yet our examination will have
shown, precisely, that neither member in this pair can be given any use
apart from the other. It also will have shown, by the same token, that
analysis of either member of such a pair must lead to an infinite regress.
('A sensory appearance is of course merely a reflection of some underlying physical thing, where by the latter we mean just something which
by definition supports sensory appearances, which themselves are, as we
say, merely reflections of. . .'.) We therefore misrepresent the use to
which the present concepts must be put, in representing the present
concepts as composing pairs at all; for, after all, a pair must consist of
two separate elements. In order to represent this use accurately, we must
somehow construe both the category of surface fact and the category of
underlying principle as being two sides of some single category. The need
to do this will require us to pass into the Doctrine of the Notion.

II.   Hegel begins the Doctrine of Essence by discussing, in *general*
terms, the Understanding's tendency to give an A-type interpretation to
the concept-pairs which we are about to consider (*EL*, §§ 112 and 114).
The Understanding tends to suppose that the essential, underlying,
enduring factor—never mind, for the moment, what specific name we
give it— can somehow have a being or standing of its own quite apart
from the various and varying surface details which it underlies. The
surface element then becomes merely the Unessential (*EL*, § 114). But
this treatment of the depth-element, Hegel suggests, involves a mistake
which actually is rather easily seen. Something essential can be essential
only to the extent that it proves essential, only to the extent that it crops
up repeatedly in one specific surface form after another. An underlying
or explanatory factor has got to have *something* to underlie and to tie
together, if it is to be itself at all. Hence the essential factor has *no*
standing or being 'on its own', if 'on its own' means 'independently from
a surface element' ('it has the unessential as its own proper seeming
[reflection] in itself', *EL,* § 114). The attempt to give it such a separate
being is really a regression to the style of thought studied in the Doctrine
of Being; Essence, in this first confused form, is still 'only charged with
the characteristics of Being' (*EL*, § 114).

III.   Hegel will wish presently to discuss some specific forms of the underlying essential factor, but he pauses, first, to make some interesting points about why it is in fact *necessary* to discuss specific forms of the underlying essential factor. These points are interesting because the Understanding has some stake in resisting them. The Understanding has some tendency—for reasons which will emerge presently—to hold on to misinterpretations of the present standpoint of manifestation-and-essence: specifically, it tends to agree that each bit of detailed surface fact is the reflection of some underlying explantory factor, but it feels that the reason why this is so is just that for any chunk of surface fact some explanatory principle could be found or formulated. In other words, the Understanding tends to feel that it is really an *empty* requirement, to say that each bit of concrete surface detail must be viewable as the reflection of underlying essence: an underlying principle can be fabricated just at will, for anything you please, and so it costs nothing to agree that some such principle can always be found.

In Hegel's language, the Understanding tends to accept the idea of Essence, but then to degrade it into the mere category of Ground. We use the category of Ground just when we are willing to settle for just any explanatory principle, no matter which, and no matter whether it is an explanatory principle invented *ad hoc* to cover a special case or not (*EL,* § 122, and *Zusatz* to § 121). Thus a person who uses the category of Ground is willing to agree that the behaviour of magnets must have some underlying explanation, and to then say that this explanation is the force of Magnetism;[3] he is willing to say that the legal code of a society can be explained as the realization of that society's moral calling, and *also* can be explained as a petty compromise between selfish interests in the society; he is willing to say that a man's behavior is justified by a principle of social morality, *and* by a principle of dog-eat-dog selfishness (*EL, Zusatz* to § 121).

Why does the Understanding favour the category of Ground? Just because this category makes the relation between surface fact and under-lying essence into a B-type relation. In using the category of Ground, it seems that we *first* identify and discuss the 'concrete surface facts' *each by itself,* and *then* go on to fabricate underlying essences; which seems to imply that each surface fact can be credited with a status or standing in its own individual right, apart from what underlying factors it may reflect. This situation is the mirror image of the situation we had a moment ago, where the Understanding tended to feel that it could discuss the underlying factor just by itself, and credit it with a standing of its own.

The weakness of the category of Ground is fairly easily seen. To say that each bit of concrete surface fact is the reflection of some underlying factor is to say that each bit of surface fact occurs for some reason, has some explanation. But there can be a reason why one thing in particular occurs, only if there is a reason why some different thing does *not* occur. An explanation explains what happens only if it rules out something else. Hence if we are to talk about underlying explanatory principles at all, we must talk about explanatory principles which rule out certain surface contents or details (*EL*, § 122, and *Zusatz* to § 121).

Hence the Understanding is wrong in feeling that some underlying principle can be fabricated for just any bit of surface content; easygoing principles such as that are not really principles at all, and do not underlie. And the Understanding is also wrong in feeling that we can discuss and identify surface contents and facts each by itself. Instead, we identify the 'concrete facts', and the 'true possibilities' (cf. *EL*, § 143 and *Zusatz*), only by referring to underlying principles which these reflect, and only by making sure that certain other surface facts—which those principles would rule out as impossible—do not obtain. And—as a final result—Hegel's intention of turning, now, to more specific forms of essence has a firm philosophical warrant.

IV.   Hegel now turns to the paired concepts of Thing and Properties (*EL*, §§ 124-130). So far Hegel has illustrated the Understanding's tendency to give an A-type interpretation to underlying essence and surface manifestations, and also its tendency to give a B-type interpretation; now Hegel will illustrate the tendency to swing back and forth from one interpretation to the other. (Hegel in fact gives a brief foretaste of this tendency in the discussion which precedes Thing and Properties, titled Existence, where he describes a tendency to see existence as being, in all cases, the reflection of certain circumstances and factors, factors which at first seem to have a selfhood (reflection-into-self) of their own but which then appear—as themselves existent—to be just reflections of further factors, etc. (*EL*, § 123 and *Zusatz*). But the same point is made in a more interesting way in the larger discussion which follows.)

Hegel begins his discussion of Thing and Properties by considering the idea of a Thing which has a colour, a taste, a smell only in relation to an observer, and which has a being or status of its own quite apart from the observer; a being of its own, therefore, apart from those properties as well (*SL*, p. 485). What will such a Thing be like? Should we conceive it as having at least a shape in its own right, and a size, and a weight; or should we conceive it as having, somehow, a being or standing of its own apart from all specifiable properties? Hegel decides to choose Kant's version of the Thing-apart-from-any-observer, and on Kant's version, this Thing-in-itself has no specifiable properties at all (*EL,* § 124). Hegel might perhaps have chosen Locke's version of the Thing-apart-from-any-observer; on Locke's version, the separate Thing does at least have shape and size. For if Hegel had chosen Locke's version, he would soon have ended up at a concept very much like Kant's in any case. The Thing, on any version of it, is an item which possesses or underlies various observable properties, but which could in principle lose any of them—even its present shape—and yet still be itself. So even if we chose Locke's version of the Thing, we should soon find ourselves asking, what is this 'itself': what is the Thing by itself, apart from all Properties (*EL,* § 125)?

'A sheer confusion', answers Hegel in *EL,* § 124; in *SL,* he states the reasons why (pp. 486-487). The Thing-by-itself is a blank unit, such as we earlier considered in Being-for-Self. It is at least distinct from other Things—after all, it is itself—but it is not distinctive in virtue of color, or smell, or shape. In fact there is 'nothing to' the Thing-by-itself by which it might back up the claim to be distinct. To say that there are many different Things-in-themselves is to make an empty claim, just words; but to say that there is only one Thing-in-itself, is to return to bare Being.

Hence the A-type interpretation, with which we have begun, must be rejected: a Thing possesses or unites certain Properties, and its whole selfhood just is the uniting of these Properties. But then—we are inclined to ask—does this not show that a B-type interpretation is in order? If the Thing is nothing but the uniter of Properties, then these properties must have some solid being or standing of their own, or else the whole conceptual picture will collapse (*EL,* § 126). Hegel therefore turns to the concept of Properties which can be discussed and conceived by themselves, without mention of some Thing which possesses them. Such a concept can be seen in our contemporary idea of sense-data. Hegel saw it in the idea, current in the science of his time, of Matters (*EL,* § 126 and *Zusatz*). Science in Hegel's time tended to analyze properties such as warmth or magnetism as being *fluids* or *stuffs,* 'caloric' or 'magnetic' 'matter'; these fluids or stuffs could (logically) exist by themselves, or come together in a unity which would then be termed a Thing (*EL,* § 127). Just so, of course, Russell held that material things were 'logically constructed' of sense data; sense-data to which, of course, our notational devices made no real difference.

But this new interpretation of Thing and Properties has a difficulty as well. If each Property is something real and self-standing in its own right, then any set of Properties—i.e., any Thing—will be just an assemblage of independent entities. Properties will have at best a spatial, and not a logical, connection with one another (*EL,* §§ 127 and 130). Each

Property will be intrinsically as simple as were the qualitative Somethings of the Doctrine of Being, and just as self-isolated; but this contradicts the basic premise of the Doctrine of Essence, that each bit of surface content is to be seen not as self-standing, but rather as the reflection of an essence (*SL,* pp. 494-496).

(Hegel's argument here could in fact be made stronger. If we were more careful in giving to each property of the Thing a being of its own, we would say that its warmth had a being of its own, its shape had a being of its own, its position had a being of its own, etc. We would not allow the warmth to possess, on its own account, a position or shape; every property everywhere would be made a separate item. But in this case we would actually have the qualitative Somethings, and the specific quanta, of the Doctrine of Being, and the earlier arguments would apply.)

V.   Hegel now begins on the middle section of the Doctrine of Essence, which he titles Appearance. Appearance, he says, is the idea of a 'ground' which 'comes forward into existence', and which is 'grounded. . .on. . .something else' (*EL,* Zusatz to § 131). What Hegel means is this. The earlier discussion of Ground showed that the underlying explanatory principles which we conceive of cannot be such as to explain just *anything*; they must instead exclude certain surface contents, and they must have a definite and specific character of their own. They must have a definite way of operating, a definite character or make-up. Hegel's present point, however, is that because the underlying principles which we discuss will have a specific character and operation, they will in certain ways themselves require to be explained. That is, we will want to ask, '*Why* does this force act at just those times, and in just those ways, that it does?'; or, 'Why does this active ingredient have the effects that it does have?'. Each of our specific underlying principles will have an operation, a nature, an existence which in some way has a further explanation, and which is a reflection of some further explanatory principle. Each will be a reflection or appearance of some further principle; hence Essence, as Hegel says, is Appearance.

We can see without further discussion that Hegel's observation here entails a new failure for A-type interpretations. A given depth-element—say, a given Force—cannot be discussed just by itself, or credited with a standing in its own right, just because each depth-element will itself be the surface reflection of some further depth-element. Now Hegel will point out that the Understanding tries to resist this new failure. The Understanding tries to get some A-interpretation to work, when faced with such a regress, by finding a 'last member' of that regress; for example, a 'first force' or a 'smallest active ingredient'.[4] But Hegel points out that this attempt really rests on a conceptual confusion.

Before considering why it is a confusion, let us look at some specific examples of such regresses. That is, let us look at some of our new, specific and definite underlying principles. One such principle, as already indicated, is the concept of Force, which is paired with the concept of Expressions. A given force operates, and expresses itself, under certain specific circumstances and in certain specific materials. Thus Magnetism is manifested in certain motions made by pieces of iron under certain circumstances. But the very specificity of a given force gives rise to the demand for certain explanations. Why does Magnetism operate just in iron and not in straw or wood? Evidently Magnetism must somehow be *bound* to iron, and kept out of wood; and the underlying explanation of this fact must lie in some further force, a 'Magnetism-directing force' (*EL, Zusatz* to § 136). Or, again, why can Magnetism operate on just these bits of iron; how do they come to be in the proximity to one another which forms the right setting for Magnetism to operate? This setting, and hence Magnetism's particular operation, must be credited to the operation of other physical forces (*EL, Zusatz* to § 136).

A different type of underlying principle—which Hegel in fact discusses before Force— is that of the Part, which casts explanatory light on some Whole. Now there are in fact applications of the concepts of Part and Whole in which neither Part nor Whole plays any explanatory role at all, and these would seem to fit under the category of Quantity; Hegel here is presumably discussing a rather different application of Part and Whole, in which Parts do explain the nature or existence of the Whole (*EL,* § 135). Thus, to give an example different from Hegel's, we often explain the nature of some commercial product by pointing to active ingredients which it contains. Hegel suggests, however, that such explanations involve a regress of their own. The whole is the way it is because it is an assemblage of certain parts; but why are these parts associated at all (*EL,* § 135)? And why is each part the way it is, or as large as it is, or in existence at all (*EL, Zusatz* to § 135, § 136)? The latter question is consistently answered only if we explain each part by reference to further parts of its own; but this then will lead to an infinite regress.

The following-out of these regresses, and of others like them, rests on a conceptual confusion, according to Hegel. It rests on the idea that there should be, somewhere down the line, some depth-element whose existence and operation makes sense strictly by itself, and which need not be understood as an offshoot, function, or dependency of something else. But this solidity is in fact not to be had. A depth element, to merit the name, must be specific; but if specific, it will at least in part be a reflection of some further depth-element.

And this point is part of a larger one, for Hegel. We have seen that there is a tendency in the Understanding to suppose there is some content to the concrete facts of the world which makes sense by itself, and which very well may, on occasion, not reflect any underlying principle at all. This tendency has been rejected in the Doctrine of Being. We also have seen that there is a tendency in the Understanding to suppose there is a content to the underlying principles and forces of the world which makes sense by itself, and which may very well not show itself in any observable reflections, any surface facts. This tendency too has now been rejected, in the discussions of the Unessential, of Ground, and of various forms of Appearance. The result is that the top line of what we have called the B-type interpretation, and the bottom line of what we have called the A-type interpretation, must both be struck out. That is, neither concrete fact nor underlying principle can be credited with a separable content in its own right. Each is intrinsically tied to the other. The intrinsic content of each lies in the role each plays in regard to the other: concrete fact is the illustrator of the depth-element, and the depth-element is explainer of concrete fact. Hence, as Hegel indicates in *EL,* § 133, and repeats in *EL,* § 151, we have a 'swinging over of content into form, and *vice versa'.* The same point is held by Hegel to show that depth-element and surface-element are not genuinely separate concepts, separate elements, at all (*EL,* § 153 and *Zusatz,* § 157, and § 158). Both surface-element and depth-element are really the complex realization of a single job, a job which might be termed 'the working of explanatory principles', or 'proving-explanatory-as-such'.

These points also explain certain hints which Hegel scatters throughout the *Zusätze* or the Doctrine of Essence. Concrete fact and underlying principles are not separable, but are just the joint realization of something which might be called 'the working of explanatory principles as such'; but this something could also be called 'the occurrence of suitable raw material for ongoing science', or even 'the occurrence of suitable raw material for ongoing practice'. The first of these labels fits because raw material for science must be such as to raise questions (it must include concrete facts of a varied and perplexing sort) and also such that these questions can be answered (the facts must ultimately reflect unifying, explanatory principles). The second of these labels fits because raw material for practice must be predictably useable (hence its behaviour must reflect underlying principles) but must also be uncooperative enough to call forth real effort (its behaviour must be a reflection of blind Forces, not of particular Purposes). Now just because both of these labels turn out to fit all forms of 'concrete fact and underlying principle', the forms of 'concrete fact and underlying principle' can be tied in with the Idea, with the open-ended project of on-going conscious endeavour. And this is why Hegel hints repeatedly that a *teleological* treatment of 'concrete fact and underlying principle' is what we must ultimately have (*EL, Zusätze* to §§ 121, 123, 131, 136, and 159).

VI. Hegel now turns to the third and final part of the Doctrine of Essence, titled Actuality, in which, he suggests, it will be more evident than before that the surface-element and the depth-element are not really separate elements at all, but are instead the joint realization of a single job: a job, namely, of explaining or proving-explanatory.[5]

Hegel begins with a brief discussion of the concept-pair Substance and Accidents. The idea of Substance is similar to the idea, considered earlier, of the Thing: a Substance is an entity which can undergo various changes, and take on various forms in varying contexts, and yet still remain itself, retain its identity. (The idea differs from the idea of a Thing in just two respects: it can make sense to suggest that there is, in the world, just *one* Substance, having of course many accidental features; and the idea can be applied not just to physical things but to God, as it was by Spinoza.) Hegel's point about Substance and Accidents is that the pair seems to invite an A-type interpretation, but that a closer examination shows that the right interpretation is what we have called an 'AB-type' interpretation. The Accidents of a Substance—the various phases and features which it acquires and loses—are supposed to be items which we can pin down, and discuss, only by reference to that underlying Substance: they are phases of it, or features of it. Substance is, as Hegel puts it, the 'absolute power' over the Accidents (*EL, § 151*). But it is equally true, as closer examination shows, that Substance needs its Accidents, and cannot be credited with a standing or being of its own apart from them. Substance can be itself, can be a deep-lying basis, only if it is the basis of something, and has something to underlie. Its own intrinsic content is really just its self-disclosure or revelation in a series of accidental phases and features (*EL, § 151*). The content of underlying Substance is inseparable from the formal role of unifying and explaining accidents; also, the content of the Accidents is inseparable from the formal role of illustrating or marking out Substance; just as, on the other hand, these formal functions are inseparable from Substances and Accidents which embody them. Thus, as Hegel says, 'there is an absolute swinging-over of form and content into one another' (*EL, § 151*).

Hegel now turns to make some similar points concerning the concept-pair, Cause and Effect. We should note that Hegel's use of these labels is rather unusual among philosophers. What Hegel means by a Cause is not some item or factor which merely *happens* to produce, and explain, some further thing, and which has a definite content in its own right apart from this production; what Hegel labels Cause is something whose very *being*, whose very intrinsic content, consists in being the producer and explainer of some definite Effect. And, similarly, what Hegel calls an Effect is something which in essence is the reflector of some particular agent or Cause. An example of what Hegel calls an Effect would be some person whose whole personality, whose very being, consisted in 'being the offspring of' some particular, and probably famous, parent. An example of Hegel's Cause would be that of some parent whose very life had no other meaning than that of 'being the progenitor of' some illustrious daughter or son.

Given these provisions, Hegel's points about Cause and Effect are easy to see. Cause and Effect are not 'two several independent existences' (*EL*, § 153), but are really a single job of 'explaining' in embodied form. There is no content to Cause by itself, and none to Effect by itself; there only are, within the single job of explaining, correlated formal roles, and Cause is the bearer of one of these, Effect of the other. Needless to say, the Understanding tends to think otherwise. When we follow the Understanding, we 'never get over the difference of the form-characteristics in their relation' (*EL*, § 153): we tend to feel that the Cause must really be something other than the Effect, and separable from the Effect; but this only launches us on another infinite regress, like the infinite regresses of Parts (*EL*, § 153). The Understanding does, indeed, sometimes rise to partial recognition of the fact that the Cause is inseparable from the Effect, and Effect from Cause; it gets so far as to think that the two are *physically* inseparable, and this thought gets expressed in the use of the category of Reciprocity (*EL*, §§ 154-155). But the true point is that we cannot even draw a *conceptual* distinction between 'Effect as it is in itself' and 'Effect as it stands towards its Cause', or between 'Cause as it is in itself' and 'Cause as it stands towards Effect'. Both Effect and Cause are, through and through, the job of 'proving explanatory'. Hence in a certain sense it is right to say that what each Cause causes is itself (*EL*, § 153); in a certain sense it is also right to say that everything which gets necessitated, brought about, is necessitated not by some alien other at all but by itself. To be under the thumb of Necessity is not bondage but Freedom (*EL*, §§ 158-159).

3

The Doctrine of the Notion

I. From the start of the Doctrine of the Notion Hegel is preparing ground for the final category or concept in the *Logic,* the only concept which will prove free from various conceptual problems which we have encountered so far. This concept is the Idea, the concept of a process or project whose end is the second-order end of there being purposive work towards specific first-order ends. Now such a project by nature involves three aspects. There must be a mass of scattered concrete facts and objects, against which particular projects can be launched; these scattered facts and objects be underlain by regularities and principles, since only so can they be mastered, only so can this or that specific purpose become achieved; and there must be conscious agents which pursue specific purposes, and which also, unknowingly or knowingly, carry out the second-order end of ongoing purposive activity for its own sake. It is this third aspect, conscious subjects, which has now to be introduced. Hence Hegel titles this third part of the *Logic,* 'Subjective Logic'.[1] The first two parts of the *Logic* are 'Objective Logic', since, as we will see, the categories studied there must all ultimately be treated as categories of object-for, raw-material-for, the successive specific purposes of conscious subjects.

At present, however, Hegel offers us only an outline of the final concept in the *Logic*; and this outline is called the Notion. The Notion is said to be the idea of an immaterial formal principle, but one which somehow is not merely formal nor merely abstract. Hegel says that the Notion, while formal, is a 'form. . .which includes, but at the same time releases from itself, the fullness of all content' (*EL, Zusatz* to § 160); and that, 'although it be abstract,. . .it is the concrete, concrete altogether. . .' (*EL,* § 169). These remarks become understandable if we reflect that the Notion will not be an underlying element, of the sort we considered in the Doctrine of Essence, but will instead be a pure function or job, much like the 'working of explanatory principles as such' which we have considered already; a job which involves in itself both concrete fact and underlying elements, while being itself an immaterial principle. In fact, as just suggested, the Notion will turn out to be the outline of a job in which this 'working of explanatory principles' is just one constituent role; and the informing purpose of this larger job will be the purpose of there being conscious endeavour as such. This is why Hegel continues the passage I quoted just above in this way: '. . .it is the concrete, concrete altogether, the Subject as such. The absolutely concrete is the mind—the notion when it *exists* as notion distinguishing itself from its objectivity, which notwithstanding the distinction still continues to be its own' (*EL*, § 164).

II.   Hegel's actual argument in the Doctrine of the Notion first gets under way, however, when Hegel returns in §§ 193-194 to topics he considered in the Doctrine of Essence. In the Doctrine of Essence Hegel was considering what we would ordinarily consider to be the main categories of the realm of objects or things: he considered the category of Thing itself, of Force and Expression, of Whole and Parts, and of Cause and Effect. What Hegel does in the present discussion is to reformulate, though not yet in final form, the conclusion to which those discussions led. Hegel suggested there that we could not credit physical facts with any content in themselves apart from the role they played in regard to underlying principles, and so, vice versa, with those underlying principles: both facts and principles were, through and through, the bearers of formal functions within the working of explanatory principles. Here Hegel wishes to re-emphasize the point that objects of every sort can ultimately be credited with no content in their own individual right, and that such content as any object has consists in a role which it embodies, a role within some job or Project. But Hegel is as yet vague about *what* job or Project he wishes to place in this role, and this forces him at times to concede that his remarks must appear somewhat stretched.[2]

Hegel begins with a preliminary mention of Leibniz, who postulated a system of separate objects but made the content of each object consist simply in the role which each object played in regard to the others (*EL*, § 194); he then turns to the far more familiar idea of Mechanism (*EL*, §§ 195-199). Mechanism is the concept of a plurality of distinct items, each of which *seems* to have a quite definite content of its own apart from any relation to the rest, and each of which seems only accidentally to occupy any particular role in relation to the rest (*EL*, § 195). The central example of this concept is, of course, a set of material objects scattered in space and colliding with each other in various ways, but Hegel also suggests that the same concept is in effect used by people who picture society as a merely external association of persons, each of whom has a complete personality or personhood in their own isolated right.[3] Hegel's point is that we ultimately must—and we certainly may—see even these scattered mechanical objects as being, through and through, only the embodiers of certain roles with regard to one another, roles within an overall Project. The mere fact that mechanical objects are spatially separate, for example, need not entail that each has a content or nature that is conceptually separate: instead we can see this spatial separateness as only a prop or ingredient in a *role* which each plays in regard to the others, and we do this when we see mechanical objects as being, intrinsically, gravitational attractors or influencers (*EL,* § 196). But into what overall job or Project would such roles by nature fit? At present, Hegel can suggest only that this overall Project is the ongoing centralizing activity of a solar system; but it seems plain that Hegel means this as only a low-level example of the sort of conceptual picture which we must ultimately frame to cover objects.

Hegel next turns to Chemism, the idea of a set of distinct chemical reagents. Here Hegel is able to argue with greater plausibility that the inner content of each such object lies in the role each plays towards other objects: for all the descriptive features of a chemical agent are affected by, and all play a role in, the interactions which that agent is such as to have with other chemical agents.[4] And not only the physical make-up of each individual chemical agent, but even the very fact of its existence, cannot be understood without reference to the place of that agent within the ongoing process of chemical interaction.[5] Hence Hegel can argue that the content of a chemical object is not separable from its role in an over-all process. But Hegel can still not give any very illuminating name to that process, and he therefore cannot be wholly successful in denying to the chemical agent a content in its own separate right. As Hegel comments, the individual chemical agent does not spontaneously involve itself in chemical interaction—it does not move itself closer to other reagents, nor alter its own make-up so as to set up a reaction with its neighbours—and this does seem to leave the chemical agent with *some* 'standing in its own right', apart from its active roles (*EL,* § 202). As Hegel points out, we still have not reached the conceptual picture which we outlined, a while back, as the Notion (*EL, Zusatz* to § 202).

III.   Hegel therefore turns to the next, and last, of his attempts to show that objects need not, and should not, be credited with a content in their own individual right, but instead both may and must be seen as having, for content, only their role in a connected Project. The concept which Hegel employs in this final attempt is that of Teleology. Hegel tells us that when we hear of Teleology, we 'must not at first, nor must we ever merely, think of' *finite* Teleology, or what Hegel also calls *external* Design (*EL,* § 204); but it appears that this is what we nonetheless do think of, according to Hegel, because Hegel introduces his comments on the right concept of Teleology by contrasting them with this concept of finite, or external, Teleology.

Let us, then, ourselves begin with the concept of finite Teleology. This concept is applied when we explain some concrete occurrence, or some concrete physical outcome, as being the work of, the doing of, some particular End or Goal. The particular End is said to 'bring itself about' through the concrete occurrence, and the concrete outcome is viewed as being 'the realization of' the End. Thus the growth of a certain layer of bark in a tree be explained—to give a ridiculous example which Hegel offers—as the achievement of the end of there being corks (*EL, Zusatz* to § 205).

The category of finite Teleology is, then, a rather unpersuasive attempt at a category of explanation, such as we studied in the Doctrine of Essence; and the weakness of the category lies in the fact that it would be a perfect candidate for what we there called a 'B-type interpretation', provided we set aside for the moment the point that neither A-type nor B-type interpretations ever really work. That is, if we consider the concrete physical objects and occurrences in which some particular End supposedly brings itself about and realizes itself, we find that these objects and occurrences certainly can be credited with a content and make-up of their own, quite apart from their incidental feature of realizing that End. The object has its own physical make-up—its own chemical or mechanical make-up—and its behaviour is chemical or mechanical behaviour; the surface-element seems definitely to make sense by itself, apart from its function of realizing or reflecting the supposedly explanatory End.[6] And the physical arrangement in which the End is said to be 'realized' is, as a chemical and mechanical arrangement, quite capable of altering or of deteriorating, i.e. of ceasing to be the realization of that End.[7]

Hegel's interest however is not in this category of finite Teleology but in what he calls 'infinite Teleology' or 'inner Design'; and the meaning of these phrases can once again best be seen if we draw a comparison with the Doctrine of Essence. In the Doctrine of Essence Hegel ended up with the position that content can be credited neither to concrete facts and objects, by themselves, nor to underlying principles, and that either element has, for content, only its role in regard to the other, roles summed together as 'the working of explanatory principles, as such'. In the present case we must likewise say, somehow, that content cannot be credited to the concrete physical event and outcome by themselves, nor (certainly) to a specific End by itself; we must somehow say, if we are to use these concepts at all, that either element has, for its content, only its role in regard to the other. These roles can be summed together as something which we might call 'the getting-realized-of-particular-Ends-as-such'. This overall process or project is itself an End of a second-order sort, and it is the central component of what Hegel calls '*infinite* Teleology'.

We have just said that the concrete physical behaviour, by some concrete object, which results in the concrete arrangement in which a particular End is realized, seems to have a content in its own right, independent of the achieving or reflecting of that End. But if we now consider this concrete behaviour and outcome as playing a role in 'the getting-realized-of-particular-Ends-as-such', we find that all of its independent content just amounts to features which qualify the concrete behaviour and outcome to hold down such a role. Let us consider it step-by-step. There can be the getting-realized-of-particular-Ends only if there is work towards this or that End; and there can be work toward this or that End only if there are suitable materials on which work can be expended. Materials on which work can be expended must be inert, i.e. they must have no tendency in themselves to realize Ends spontaneously, but only to the extent that work is expended on them (*EL,* § 209); they must also behave in accordance with laws, since work can be work only if it can at some point claim responsibility for a completed outcome, and there is no responsibility for an outcome brought about magically or spontaneously or unpredictably, etc. Hence the getting-realized-of-particular-Ends involves in itself the existence of material objects which behave in accordance with blind, mechanical or chemical, laws. But to say this is just to say that what seemed a moment ago to be independent content in the object which is said to realize some particular End—namely, the mechanical-chemical nature of that object—is just what qualifies objects as role-bearers in the getting-realized-of Ends (*EL,* § 212).

We also noted, a moment ago, that the concrete physical outcome in which a particular End is (supposedly) realized is such, by nature, as to deteriorate, to cease to realize that End: clocks and houses follow the laws of physics, not of utility, and cease after a time to function as clocks or houses at all (*SL,* p. 750). In so doing, however, they also set up new needs or Ends, and become new material for new work. Hence the physical and non-teleological character of concrete outcomes is precisely something that qualifies them as role-players in the ongoing getting-realized-of-Ends-as-such.

Hence Hegel comments:

> . . .In the fact that the [sc. particular] End achieved is characterized only as a Means and a material [sc. for the getting-achieved-of-Ends-as-such], this object, viz. the teleological, is there and then put as implicitly null, and only 'ideal'. This being so, the antithesis between form and content has also vanished. While the End by the removal and absorption of all form-characteristics coalesces with itself, the form as self-identical is thereby put as a content, so that the notion, which is the action of form, has only itself for content. Through this process, therefore, there is made explicitly manifest what was the notion of design: viz. the implicit unity of subjective and objective is now realised. And this is the Idea. [*Zusatz*] This finitude of the End consists in the circumstance, that, in the process of realizing it, the material, which is employed as a means, is only externally subsumed under it and made conformable to it. But, as a matter of fact, the object is the notion implicitly: and thus when the notion, in the shape of End, is realised in the object, we have but the manifestation of the inner nature of the object itself. Objectivity is thus, as it were, only a covering under which the notion lies concealed. Within the range of the finite we can never see or experience that the End has been really secured. The consummation of the infinite End, therefore, consists merely in removing the illusion which makes it seem yet unaccomplished (*EL,* § 212 and *Zusatz*).

Hegel's present discussion might have been given even more interest if Hegel had added one closely connected point. Thus far Hegel has argued that physical objects may be seen as being simply raw material for the pursuit of this or that specific End. Hegel might have added that these objects may be seen as being raw material, not simply for the pursuit of this or that practical End, i.e. raw material for *physical* work, but also as being raw material for cognitive Ends, i.e. for ongoing *cognitive* work. This is so because the same inert independence which makes physical good targets for the expenditure of physical work also—as the point that physical objects have a make-up quite independent of any activity of figuring them out—makes them good targets for the expenditure of cognitive work. And it is so because any time we win cognitive mastery over some one physical object—any time we find out what caused it, what laws it follows, etc.—we also find that physical object passing us over to new cognitive needs, as yet unfilled—e.g., to questions such as 'what caused that cause?', or 'what law governs the antecedents of this law?', etc. Such additions would have given greater interest to Hegel's discussion since they would have left Hegel saying that any physical object may and must be seen as a role-player in the getting-pursued-of-Ends-practical-*and-cognitive*. To emphasize practical ends alone is to suggest that all physical objects must be seen as tools, which in view of the vastness of space, and the apparent perpetual uselessness of many objects, seems awkard. But the incompleteness in Hegel's present discussion will, in any case, be made good when we arrive at what Hegel calls 'the Absolute Idea'.

IV. Hegel now begins on the third and final section of the Doctrine of the Notion, titled The Idea. Here he will at last indicate the place which conscious subjects, and conscious subjectivity, have in his philosophy. Hegel's latest discussion on Teleology has shown that we may—and all the discussions prior to that have shown that we must—treat concrete objects and facts as having, for content, only their role in a complex and self-perpetuating Project. This Project, I have suggested, could be called the getting-realized-of-particular-Ends; more fully, given the addition mentioned just above, it could be called the getting-realized-of-particular-ends-both-practical-and-cognitive, and in this way our Project will turn out to include the one of which we spoke earlier, viz. the working of explanatory principles. What Hegel now wants to urge is that this Project, by whatever name, can be realized in objects and in material laws, or in objects and in material ends, only if also realized in a third element or content as well, namely the activity of conscious subjects. The reason why this claim is important is that the arguments thus far have indicated that the only real world that can genuinely be discussed or conceived is a world which embodies this project, i.e. embodies the Idea.

Now it might seem that no argument is really needed to show that conscious subjectivity occupies a necessary role within the Project which we are considering. For how could there be purposive work towards this or that specific goal unless there were conscious agents to perform that work? And has not conscious subjectivity been provided for—or smuggled in—by talk of the working of explanatory principles? But, as to the question about purposive work, Hegel did point out that achievement of this or that finite End may be discussed even when no conscious agent, who intends that end, is present. And, as to the working of explanatory principles, might such principles not work—in the sense of underlying concrete events—even without actually providing explanation or illumination to any conscious minds? Hegel has in any case a further argument, or partial argument, on which to rely. This argument he does not in fact set out until later, in the transition from Life to what Hegel calls Cognition; but it will be useful to sketch that argument now. We have seen already that Hegel's Project has what could be called a 'second-order' end; its end is a purpose about first-order purposes, and it is realized in the pursuing of this first-order purpose and of that and of that, in an open-ended series. Specific purposes are pursued, but the real goal in each case is the general one of the pursuing as such of specific purposes. Hegel's argument is that such pursuit of a second-order purpose can genuinely be realized only if there is something in the realization which treats the pursuit of the first-order ends as open-ended; something which somehow makes evident in its purposive behaviour that its real aim is the universal of purposive activity as such. But such a treatment, such an indication, is possible only through the linguistic and conceptual behaviour of conscious subjects.[8] These, therefore, form a necessary element in the realization of Hegel's Project. Indeed, Hegel will now find it possible to say that his Project is just the Project of there being ongoing conscious purposiveness, as such; that is, the Project is Mentality; that is, the Project is to be called Mind.

In the first three sections of this last part of the Doctrine of the Notion, however, Hegel provides us with only the statement that—not really with the explanation why—his project involves in itself all content of all objects (all Objectivity) and also is a principle of Mind or Subjectivity. He begins by telling us that the Idea is 'the absolute unity of the Notion and objectivity' (*EL*, § 213), and so we see that the Idea includes objectivity in itself; he then tells us that 'the Idea is *in the first place* only the one universal *substance*; but its developed and genuine actuality is to be as a *subject* and in that way as mind' (*EL*, § 213). These assertions might seem to raise questions since it might seem—if one forgot for the moment some of Hegel's earlier points—that the principle of objectivity, and the principle of subjectivity, were quite distinct. But Hegel comments that this distinction, drawn by the Understanding, is not the final fact which the Understanding supposes (*EL*, § 214). It is true that resistant objective arrangements confront the endeavours of conscious subjects as a resistant other, an alien material; but in doing so objective arrangements are precisely realizing the project of there being subjective purposiveness, and to realize this is their whole calling.

> The idea itself is the dialectic which forever divides and distinguishes the self-identical from the differentiated, the subjective from the objective, the finite from the infinite, soul from body. . . .The Idea is the dialectic which again makes the mass of understanding and diversity understand its finite nature and pseudo-independence in its productions, and which brings the diversity back to unity. Since this double movement is not separate or distinct in time, nor indeed in any other way—otherwise it would be only a repetition of the abstract understanding—the Idea is the eternal vision of itself in the other,—notion which in its objectivity *has* carried out *itself*—object which is inward design, essential subjectivity (*EL*, § 214).

Hegel then adds, lest the point should somehow have been missed, that the Idea is a process, and is the process of subjectivity (*EL*, § 215).

V. Hegel now proceeds to discuss in greater detail just what the Idea involves. He begins with what he calls an 'immediate' form of the Idea, namely the concept of Life. The concept of Life is the concept of a self-perpetuating and self-sustaining purposive system, rather like the Idea proper, but it also is immediate in the sense of being in some ways the concept of a simple quality, namely the organic, quite separate from the non-organic, and not having the all-pervasive universality of the Idea proper.

But despite this qualitative cast, the idea of Life can quite readily be seen to resemble what we have called the Idea. To begin with the inner side of the living organism—its physiology—it can be held that the whole content and character of each organ lies in the role which each plays within the organism as a whole. Thus, as Aristotle points out, what makes a hand a hand is not its having a certain descriptive appearance, a qualitative make-up, as such; it is the performing of a certain role (*EL*, § 216). The role of each organ is, in general terms, the same: each functions so as to maintain health and functioning in the organism as a whole; and hence each organ can be seen as motivated by a purpose of there being ongoing purposive activity as such. An organ contributes to ongoing organic operation by restoring or nourishing or repairing some other organ, but it is also the case that organs contribute to ongoing organic operation by providing targets for that operation, that is, by becoming exhausted or by breaking down, etc. Hence, as Hegel says, the living organism by nature 'makes a split on its own self': certain organs break down, get in the way of others, and call for restoring and repairing activities from others (*EL*, § 218). The repairing organs function as means, with the end being restored operation in the organs that have broken down; on the other hand those organs, by breaking down, have enabled the repairing organs to work, and so have served as means to the end of the operation of the repairing organs. Hence, as Hegel puts it, 'all the members are reciprocally momentary means as well as momentary ends' (*EL*, § 216).

Similar points emerge if we consider the outer side of the organism, namely its behaviour. The organism has needs and purposes which it must satisfy by manipulating an indifferent, external environment. But the organism characteristically adjusts its needs so that the environment, indifferent as it is, ends up blindly realizing those needs; that is, the organism adapts, it harnesses the chemical and mechanical properties of its surroundings to its own purposes (*EL*, § 219). And the organism also characteristically creates for itself fresh needs, by using up or digesting its earlier acquisitions. Both facts show that the real guiding purpose of the organism is just the ongoing-pursuit-of-specific-Ends-in-general, rather that the more specific purpose of gaining *this* particular end or *that*.[9]

There is room, then, to discern a second-order end in the purposive activities of the living organism. It nevertheless is not possible to see, in these activities alone, an adequate embodiment of that radically general Project, which is the Idea. The Idea, as has been indicated, is a process in which the real purpose of all these pursuings is simply the pursuit as such of ends. But for such a process to be fully realized, fully embodied, there must occur in the embodiment some element which indicates the generality of the aim. It is not enough that there be agents that pursue one specific end after another, in open-ended succession, and it certainly is not enough that there be agents that pursue specific ends having the monotonous sameness of an animal's characteristic ends;[10] what is needed is that there be agents that by their behaviour treat this succession of ends *as* open-ended and as, in principle, wholly various in content. And this requirement is tied, in turn, to another. An agent that does pursue an end which is general, and which can by nature be promoted in an open variety of specific undertakings, pursues an end that can by nature be promoted by other agents as well. Others too can do 'what that agent is about'. Hence agents that treat their end as thus general must also treat themselves as being replaceable: they must act as if all that matters in their lives is something general, instantiable equally well in other lives. Either requirement entails that there must be, in any full realization of the Idea, agents that show a responsiveness to universals and general meanings, as such. And this in turn entails that there must be agents that possess conceptual and linguistic behaviours, i.e. conscious rational agents. Animals may, with some stretching, be said to show a general concern with purposive activity as such, in fostering such activity not only in themselves but also in mates and offspring (*EL*, § 220). But there is no warrant for saying that animals genuinely treat the purposive activity of these close relations as cases of a universal. Likewise, animals do not treat themselves as replaceable. Animals merely *are* replaced, they merely die.[11] Only linguistic agents treat themselves as instances of a universal: this occurs, Hegel feels, in the use of the term 'I'. For it is a function of the very concept or word 'I', that a person uses it rightly and with understanding only if he is set to recognize that there should be other 'I's, equally as genuine as himself (*EL, Zusatz* (1) to § 24).

Hegel therefore now takes up the position that his Project of there being the ongoing pursuit of goals can get fully realized only if that realization involves linguistic, rational conscious agents (*EL*, § 222). The agency of these agents is discussed under the concepts of Cognition and of Volition, and is then set in its true light in the concluding discussion of what Hegel calls the Absolute Idea.

VI.   The points which Hegel makes in the paragraphs on Cognition and
Volition are connected with points which we have already considered in
the Doctrine of Being and the Doctrine of Essence. We have seen that
there is a natural tendency to suppose that the concrete facts of the world
are brute facts, which at best happen to reflect underlying explanatory
principles; also, that it is natural to suppose that the deep-lying forces
and laws of the world may very well not show themselves in observable
manifestations. Such views of the world are connected with a view on our
own approach towards the world, as Hegel now points out: they suggest
that the materials we tackle, each time we seek to gain some particular
insight or cognitive mastery, are wholly indifferent to our undertaking,
and may even be hostile to it (*EL,* § 226 and *Zusatz*). Such an idea is
involved in the usual conception of Cognition. It is sometimes even
sharpened by philosophers into the idea that all efforts to gain insight
inevitably distort the object which we are considering—since such efforts
involve 'the reception of it into categories which. . .remain external to
it'—and that the real truth is therefore 'an inaccessible goal in a world of
its own' (*EL,* § 226). On a truer picture of the materials which Cognition
tackles, however, it becomes clear that no distortion is involved. It lies in
the very nature of facts that facts happen for a reason, i.e. are
necessitated by principles; but then it lies in the very nature of facts that
facts can be understood and predicted, i.e. made the subject of what
Hegel calls a Demonstration (*EL,* § 232).

Hegel next considers, under the rather misleading title of Volition, our
practical approach to the world; in particular, *moral* practice. At what
goal, at what good, does moral practice aim? Kant and Fichte both
suggested that the highest good is moral practice itself, but they then
failed to provide an account of the concrete factual setting for moral
practice. Should we wish that some day this factual setting should be
completely made over by moral practice into a perfect world? But then
what would become of moral *practice?* The truth is that an imperfect and
indifferent factual world is an integral element in any realization of the
highest good, since only so can there be material for continued moral
efforts (*EL,* §§ 234-235).

VII.   Hegel therefore moves to the final concept in the *Logic,* which he
titles the Absolute Idea. The Absolute Idea is the idea of a subjective
purposiveness like the moral practice which we just considered, in that its
aim is just the general one of ongoing purposiveness as such, but unlike
both moral practice and cognition in that it recognizes the particular
materials on which it directs its particular efforts as being, in their
innermost essence, the same project which it fundamentally is. Hegel

comments that the Absolute Idea is like the principle of Life, just because it is a purposiveness which is unworried about the otherness of the materials which it tackles; but it also is unlike life, since it is a purposiveness embodied in agents who treat themselves as being, in their innermost content, something general (*EL, Zusatz* to § 236). Hence Hegel says that the Absolute Idea is a universal or 'notion whose target (*Gegenstand*) is the Idea as such, and for which the material (*Objekt*) is Idea' (*EL*, § 236). Or, as Hegel writes in the *Science of Logic,*

> The Absolute Idea has shown itself to be the identity of the theoretical and the practical Idea. Each of these by itself is still one-sided, possessing the Idea itself only as a sought-for beyond and an unattained goal; each, there-fore, is a *synthesis of endeavour,* and has, but equally has *not,* the Idea in it; each passes from one thought to the other without bringing the two together, and so remains fixed in their contradiction. The absolute Idea, as the rational Notion that in its reality meets only with itself, is by virtue of this immediacy of its objective identity, on the one hand the return to *life*; but it has no less sublated this form of its immediacy, and contains within itself the highest degree of opposition. The Notion is not merely *soul,* but free subjective Notion that is for itself and therefore possesses *personality*—the practical, objective Notion determined in and for itself which, as person, is impenetrable atomic subjectivity—but which, nonethe-less, is not exclusive individuality, but explicitly *universality* and *cognition,* and in its other has *its own* objectivity for its object. All else is error, confusion, opinion, endeavour, caprice and transitoriness; the absolute Idea alone is *being,* imperishable *life, self-knowing truth,* and is *all truth.* It is the sole subject matter and content of philosophy. Since it contains *all* determinateness within it, and its essential nature is to return to itself through its self-determination or particularization, it has various shapes, and the business of philosophy is to cognize it in these. Nature and spirit are in general different modes of presenting *its existence,* art and religion its different modes of apprehending itself and giving itself an adequate exist-ence (*SL,* p. 824).

In the Encyclopedia *Logic,* however, Hegel is especially concerned with this question: can we, as philosophical readers of the *Logic,* claim that the concepts which we have been tackling are themselves just embodiments of the same project which *we* embody? The usual con-ception of philosophy, and of philosophical method, suggests otherwise. The usual conception suggests that the philosopher confronts topics distinct from himself, and tackles these topics by means of yet a third thing, philosophical method (*SL,* pp. 825-827). But Hegel indicates that this picture should be avoided. Philosophical method, if we are going to use the concept, is the self-pursuing cognitive purposiveness which the philosopher embodies. And this project of cognitive purposiveness is

equally embodied in the one-sided ideas which provide material for philosophical sense-making, namely the categories which we have studied
thus far. Philosophical activity requires the apparent separations which
the Understanding draws, if it is to be able to dig beneath these and
reinterpret them. Hence philosophical 'method is not an extraneous
form, but the soul and notion of the content, from which it is only
distinguished, so far as the dynamic elements of the notion even on their
own part come in their own specific character to appear as the totality of
the notion' (*EL*, § 243). In dealing with the one-sided categories of the
Logic, we are not dealing with an other, but with an embodiment of the
very activity which we are; the Logical Idea 'is the *noesis noeseos* which
Aristotle long ago termed the supreme form of the Idea' (*EL, Zusatz* to §
236). But we must not suppose that philosophical purposiveness is the
only form of the Absolute Idea; Hegel clearly intends something more
general. 'The highest, most concentrated point is the *pure personality*
which, solely through the absolute dialectic which is its nature, no less
embraces and holds everything within itself' (*SL,* p. 841).

4

The Logic and the Mind-Body Problem

I.   This monograph began with the suggestion that the line of argument, which we now have traced through the three divisions of the *Logic*, can provide support for a position on certain central aspects of the mind-body problem which is both different from, and superior to, the main positions favoured in contemporary discussion. The purpose of this final Part is to state just what this alternative position is, and just how the line of thought traced here supports it. The support provided is, in general, indirect: the *Logic* grounds arguments to the effect that the existing positions on mind and body are not simply inferior to some position, but flatly untenable; any position on mind and body consonant with the *Logic* will, then, be a superior position. For this reason, and for the reason that objections to existing positions on mind and body emerge far more readily from the *Logic* than does the characterization of a positive alternative, this Part will deal with the topics indicated in reverse order. It first will set forth the reasons for thinking that existing alternatives to a Hegelian position on mind and body are unacceptable; it then will indicate, by quotation and inference, what the Hegelian position is.

The mind-body problem is many-faceted, and it is important to begin by specifying just what those central aspects are on which the *Logic* may be held to furnish a better answer than do contemporary approaches. Contemporary theories on mind and body are motivated, at least in large measure, by the conviction that the behaviour of persons can in principle be predicted and explained by use of laws of neurophysics. This conviction provokes theories precisely because it seems certain that the behaviour of persons can also be explained, and predicted with appreciable accuracy, by use of laws of psychology. Now it appears, at least initially, that the occurrences which make up human behaviour get carved up along quite different joints—to use Aristotle's metaphor—when placed under predicates of neurophysics, from the way they get carved up when placed under predicates of psychology: the question, then, is how both such seemingly different systems of carving can possess genuine predictive and explanatory power. Existing positions on mind and body are, at least largely, attempts to answer just this question. It is to this question, I argue, that the *Logic* provides an answer superior to the existing ones.

The most important contemporary rival to the Hegelian answer is—as the discussions below will indirectly show—the answer provided by eliminative materialism. Eliminative materialism contends that while it may be convenient or customary to speak as if events occurred which consisted in the satisfaction of this or that predicate of psychology, no such events ever really do occur. The predicates of psychology are not, in other words, real predicates at all. And hence the question of two-way explainability does not really arise, at least not for the class of real events: all that *really* occurs, whenever there is the behaviour of persons, are events predictable and explainable solely by use of neurophysics (and of other departments of physics). To this important position we have already seen Hegel provide an important objection. For the whole argument which we have drawn from the *Logic* is, among other things, an objection to eliminative materialism: Hegel's contention, as we have seen, is that the concepts which serve to designate physical occurrences and operators can have sound and stable use only if used in an overall conceptual scheme in which an equally genuine use is assigned for concepts which depict rational, intentional agenthood. Eliminative materialism maintains that an ideal conceptual scheme or language would use physical predicates to designate all occurrences and objects which figure in the behaviour of persons, and would use psychological predicates nowhere. But if Hegel's argument is correct, such a conceptual scheme could not actually be employed at all: the attempt to employ it would either involve an unacknowledged reintroduction of concepts depicting rational agency, or would entangle itself in sense-cancelling absurdities of a conceptual sort, vicious infinite regresses, etc.

This objection to eliminative materialism is the touchstone of the present discussion of contemporary rivals to the Hegelian position on mind and body. The position most widely discussed, in current debates on mind and body, is *non*-eliminative materialism: yet what I argue, in the next two sections, is that non-eliminative materialism must coincide, in one crucial contention, with eliminative materialism, and hence that the *Logic* can be held to provide at least the basis for an objection against non-eliminative materialism as well. Concerning the third chief rival to the Hegelian position on mind and body, namely dualism, not much need be said. Dualism responds to our central question by maintaining that it only seems as if a single system of behaviour yields to prediction, and explanation, by the use of two very different families of predicates.

In fact the behaviour of persons is not one system of behaviour, but two: there is the behaviour of a spiritual substance, and the behaviour of a material substance; and each of these systems yields to prediction and explanation by use of only one family of predicates. The two systems of behaviour, dualism adds, appear to be one only because the two substances are conjoined. To this position there is a fairly obvious objection: no independent justification is offered for asserting that the behaviour of persons is a compound of two different systems of behaviour, or that persons are conjunctions of two different substances. Frustration in the attempt, to explain how what seems to be one system of behaviour can be thus doubly explainable, may incline us to want some argument for just these assertions. But dualism exhibits nothing as constituting such an argument beyond this frustration itself. Thus the answer provided by dualism has an *ad hoc* character which qualifies it only as a last resort.

II.   Non-eliminative materialism is the position that at least some predicates of psychology are real predicates, and are really satisfied in the actual world, but that the satisfactions of these predicates are invariably mere functions of satisfactions of predicates of physics (including neurophysics), and hence yield to prediction and explanation by laws of physics. Non-eliminative materialism thus addresses our central question by arguing that the predicates of psychology are not, in fact, a different family of predicates—or are not, at least, an independent family of predicates—from the predicates of physics. But important differences exist between the specific forms which non-eliminative materialism can take. Considerations raised recently by Fodor and others suggest that non-eliminative materialism becomes a highly implausible position when construed as the thesis that for each predicate of psychology, there is some *one* predicate of physics, such that satisfaction of the former is, with nomological necessity, a mere function of satisfaction of the latter.[1] These same considerations suggest that non-eliminative materialism avoids this implausibility when construed, more modestly, as the thesis that each individual satisfaction of a predicate of psychology is a mere function of some individual satisfaction of *some* predicate *or other* of physics. The points raised by Fodor are, moreover, central for the argument to be made by the present discussion itself. They ground, by way of a different argument, the contention that non-eliminative materialism must, in its only plausible version, coincide in one crucial respect with eliminative materialism. This discussion must therefore begin with Fodor's points.

Fodor's central contention is a denial that there can be any nomological coextension between at least some predicates of psychology, and any predicates of physics; Fodor approaches this point, however, by way of the more modest suggestion that there is no actual coextension between at least some predicates of some special sciences, and proper predicates of physics. And it will be best for us to follow him in this approach. Economics, then—to take Fodor's own example—is one special science in which, one might hope, fairly rigorous laws are in principle available. Imaginably, one law of economics might concern monetary exchanges in certain specific economic circumstances. But what predicates of physics—Fodor invites us to ask—might be coextensive with 'is a monetary exchange' (or with 'is a monetary exchange in thus-and-such economic circumstances')? Simpleminded considerations suggest that actual instantiations of 'is a monetary exchange' will satisfy wildly varying descriptions under the ordinary predicates of physics: 'Some monetary exchanges involve strings of wampum. Some involve dollar bills. Some involve signing one's name to a check.'[2] What follows is not that no predicate of physics is coextensive with 'is a monetary exchange', since some elaborately disjunctive predicate of physics surely is coextensive with it; but rather that the predicate which is coextensive with 'is a monetary exchange' will not be a predicate proper to physics itself. No law of physics, that is, will incorporate this wildly disjunctive predicate in either its antecedent or its consequent.

Similar suggestions, we may note, could also be made concerning predicates of psychology inself. The laws of a fully developed psychology would, presumably, concern types of overt action, types of perceptual observation, and the like. Possibly the types discussed would be more precisely delimited than are the types discerned by such everyday predicates as 'sitting down', 'threatening with one's fists', 'hearing one's name called', 'seeing that a car is coming'; it nonetheless seems likely that certain similarities would exist between the predicates employed in a fully developed psychology, and such predicates as these. Each of these predicates is instantiated in musculo-skeletal events, or else in stimulations of sensory receptors, which satisfy widely varying descriptions under the ordinary predicates of physiology and neurophysics; it is reasonable, then, to assume that the same events satisfy widely varying descriptions even under the predicates of a highly advanced and highly unified physics. But if the predicates of every-day psychology are, as these reflections suggest, coextensive only with rather elaborately disjunctive predicates of physics, then it also is reasonable to suppose that even the predicates of a fully developed psychology will be coextensive only with rather elaborately disjunctive predicates—that is, with non-proper predicates—of physics.

Fodor's central observation, however, is a point not simply about actual coextension with predicates of physics, but about nomological coextension with predicates of physics. Non-eliminative materialism, in the version which Fodor wishes to reject, contends that satisfaction of any proper predicate of psychology is, by natural law, coincident with the satisfaction of some one predicate of physics. For it is just this fact which—on this particular version of non-eliminative materialism—explains why the laws of physics, which govern and explain satisfactions of the predicates of physics, also are laws which govern and explain satisfactions of the predicates of psychology. But can it in fact be maintained, plausibly, that there is a coextension which is *nomological* between each predicate of psychology and some predicate or other of physics—even, indeed, with some wildly disjunctive predicate of physics? If we consider a parallel question about the predicates of economics, the answer would seem to be No.[3] Over the course of the world's history, the predicate 'is a monetary exchange' will end up being coextensive with some elaborately complex predicate of physics. Each monetary exchange, that is, which occurs in the world will satisfy one or another of the physical descriptions combined in just that disjunctive predicate. But is it plausible to suggest, even so, that every monetary exchange which occurs in the world had to, or has to, satisfy just that disjunctive predicate? Is it plausible to assert that 'had this disjunctive predicate not been satisfied here, there could not have been a monetary exchange here' is a truth for all 'heres'? Intuitively, at least, it seems not.

Turning, now, to the predicates of psychology in particular, Fodor indicates that more than just intuition grounds a similar negative answer. It has widely been argued that the predicates of psychology are nomologically coextensive with functional-state descriptions. Dispute has, indeed, been raised as to whether the particular predicates of psychology which serve to attribute sensations to subjects—e.g. 'is experiencing severe pain', 'experiences the "raw feel" of redness'—are nomologically coextensive with any functional-state descriptions.[4] But concerning the predicates which serve to attribute intentional states to subjects—e.g. 'believes that p', 'hopes that q'—dispute has not even been attempted. Now it seems quite certain, as Fodor points out, that each such functional-state description is not nomologically coextensive with any predicate of physics.[5] For any one such functional-state description can be satisfied by automata satisfying *limitlessly various* physical descriptions. The arguments in favour of functionalism, therefore, are arguments to the effect that at least some predicates of psychology—those, namely, which depict intentional states—are not coextensive with any finite disjunctive predicates of physics, however elaborate these may be.

III. The only plausible version of non-eliminative materialism, then, is the version which was mentioned second above. On this second version, the satisfaction of each predicate proper to psychology is, in each individual instance, merely a function of some individual satisfaction of some predicate of physics or other; no claim is made that there is some one predicate of physics, such that satisfaction of the given predicate of psychology is, in each instance, a function of satisfaction of just that predicate of physics. It nonetheless is held, on this second version of non-eliminative materialism, that satisfactions of the predicates of psychology yield to prediction and explanation by the laws of physics. For the laws of physics predict and explain those satisfactions of physical predicates, to which individual satisfactions of predicates of psychology are tied.

The contention of the present section is that non-eliminative materialism can be defended, in this second version, only if it is buttressed by a claim which is central to eliminative materialism as well. The objection against which the second version of non-eliminative materialism requires defence begins to emerge as soon as one considers more closely the claim that each individual satisfaction of any predicate of psychology is merely a function of, or is tied to, some individual satisfaction of some predicate of physics. Formally, it is possible to interpret these phrases in either of two ways. They can be interpreted as meaning that each individual satisfaction of each predicate of psychology is an occurrence distinct from any individual satisfaction of any predicate of physics, but bound up by natural law with some individual satisfaction of some predicate of physics. Or they can, alternatively, be interpreted as meaning that each individual satisfaction of each predicate of psychology is—is identical with—some individual satisfaction of some predicate of physics. Only the second of these interpretations accurately reflects the views of actual exponents of this second form of non-eliminative materialism. And the reason for this unanimity becomes apparent quite quickly if we ask just what sort of natural law it might be, that would bind a given individual satisfaction of some predicate of psychology with some individual satisfaction of some predicate of physics. If a given satisfaction of some predicate of psychology is an occurrence distinct from any individual satisfaction of a predicate of physics, as the former interpretation maintains, then the predicate by which that given satisfaction were subsumed under a natural law could not be any predicate proper to physics. It would have to be a predicate of psychology, or else some predicate nomologically coextensive with some predicate of psychology. But, as the discussion of the last section indicated, no predicate of physics itself—no proper predicate of physics, nor even any elaborately disjunctive predicate of physics—is nomologically coextensive with any predicate of psychology. Hence the predicate by which the hypothesized natural law subsumed the given individual satisfaction of a predicate of psychology, and bound that occurrence to some individual satisfaction of some predicate of physics, could not be a predicate of physics. The hypothesized natural law would therefore not be, itself, a law of physics. And this consequence contradicts the contention, central to all forms of non-eliminative materialism, that satisfactions of the predicates of psychology yield to prediction and explanation by use of the laws of physics. For this consequence amounts to the position that satisfactions of the predicates of psychology are governed, given circumstances determined by laws of physics, by laws irreducible to the laws of physics.

Non-eliminative materialism in this second form must therefore embrace the view that each individual satisfaction of each predicate of psychology is identical with some individual satisfaction of some predicate of physics. It is not surprising that this is Fodor's own view.[6] Yet the observations made by Fodor, and recounted in the previous section, provide what appears, at least, to be a quick and decisive refutation of this thesis of token event-identity. Suppose that some individual (or token) satisfaction of some psychological predicate P is in fact held to be an occurrence identical with some individual satisfaction of some physical predicate Q. Assuming that psychology is a viable science, there will be some law of psychology which governs satisfaction of P (as a type of occurrence); the antecedents of this law will themselves be proper predicates of psychology. But we have seen, in the preceding section, reason to think that no predicates of psychology are nomologically coextensive with any predicates of physics; and thus, in particular, that the predicates of psychology which pick out causal antecedents of satisfactions of P are not nomologically coextensive with any predicates of physics. More particularly, these predicates will not be nomologically coextensive with those predicates of physics—whatever they are—which pick out causal antecedents of satisfactions of the physical predicate Q. But what this entails is that causal antecedents for satisfaction of P might—so far as nomological possibility goes—continue to obtain in the particular place and time where our given individual satisfaction of P is now, even though causal antecedents for satisfaction of Q no longer obtained there. That is, P itself might continue to be satisfied in that place, through continuous stretches of time, even though Q were no longer satisfied there. And it *seems*, at least, that this same result can quite legitimately be paraphrased as the assertion that this individual satisfaction of P might quite well continue, even though this individual satisfaction of Q were to cease. Of course the converse claim can, with equal justice, be made: namely, that it is nomologically possible that this individual satisfaction of Q should continue, even though this individual satisfaction of P were to cease. If, however, either assertion is in fact legitimate, then either is fatal to the position that this individual satisfaction of P is an occurrence identical with this individual satisfaction of Q. For it is not nomologically possible—it is not even logically possible—that one and the same individual occurrence should both continue, and cease, at the same time.

It is in this way, then, that the observations of the preceding section appear to provide a quick and decisive objection against the thesis of token event-identity. And if this appearance is accurate, then—since that thesis is required by the only plausible version of non-eliminative materialism—the observations of the preceding section provide a quick and decisive objection against non-eliminative materialism itself. Now there is, in fact, a way in which the thesis of token event-identity, and with it non-eliminative materialism, can be defended against the objection just raised. But it is just here that the defence of non-eliminative materialism must involve endorsement of a position central to eliminative materialism. For consider just where the objection, raised above, becomes vulnerable to counter-attack. It becomes vulnerable just at the point where it paraphrases the result 'it is nomologically possible that satisfaction of psychological predicate P should continue, just where the given individual satisfaction of P now occurs, even though satisfaction of physical predicate Q should cease there', as the assertion 'it is nomologically possible that this satisfaction of P should continue, even though this satisfaction of Q should cease'. It is arguable that the two propositions are by no means equivalent. For it is arguable that the occurrence designated by 'this satisfaction of P' is an occurrence which could quite well continue, even though there should cease to be, in the relevant place, satisfaction of P; in other words, that the occurrence designated by 'this satisfaction of P' does not need to *be* a satisfaction of P in order to be itself. And by the same token it is arguable that the occurrence which might fail to continue, even though satisfaction of P should continue in the relevant place; or in other words that continued satisfaction of P in the relevant place is not a sufficient condition for the occurrence designated by 'this satisfaction of P' to continue as itself. If such contentions as these are argued, the objection raised above is rendered harmless. For in that case the point that satisfaction of P might continue here, even though satisfaction of Q should cease here, need not be conceded to entail that the occurrence designated by 'this satisfaction of P' might continue, even though the occurrence designated by 'this satisfaction of Q' should cease. But the only basis on which such contentions could be argued is the position that continued satisfaction of* P, in a given place, does not by itself amount to a real continuing of some real occurrence; and, conversely, that cessation in satisfaction of P, in some given place, does not by itself amount to a real cessation of some real occurrence. And to take this position is to say that the predicate P is not, in its own right, a real predicate; it is to say that P is a predicate not qualified for picking out real continuings, and real ceasings, in the world. This position is therefore equivalent to a central claim of *eliminative* materialism. It is directly contradicted by the argument which has been drawn, in this monograph, from the *Logic*; for what that argument entails, among other things, is that in any sound conceptual scheme, an equally genuine role is assigned for concepts which serve to depict the rational, intentional agency of agents, as is assigned for concepts which serve to depict physical occurrences and operators.

IV. The *Logic* therefore provides at least the basis for serious objections to the more persuasive contemporary answers on our central question of two-way explainability. But it further can be argued that the *Logic* furnishes a positive alternative to those contemporary answers.

The answer furnished by the *Logic* differs not just in content, but also in approach, from the materialist answers which we have just examined in detail. But the results of our examination can serve to indicate just how, and why, such a different approach is justified. The question of two-way explainability was formulated, at the outset of the present Part, as the question why the behaviour of persons yielded to prediction and explanation by the use of what seem to be two very different families of predicates, viz. the predicates of psychology and the predicates of physics (including neurophysics). The approach to this question which is taken by materialism is to view it as being a question about a certain system of physical, and neurophysical, events: the question, in this case, is 'how can it be explained that the predicates of psychology have predictive and explanatory applicability to this system of events?'. And as our discussions thus far have suggested, materialists have generally envisioned answers to this question falling into either of two main types. Some materialists have felt that a single answer could in principle be provided, by neurophysics, for the explanatory applicability of each proper predicate of psychology, taken individually. Such a view was in effect discussed above, in considering the first version of non-eliminative materialism; for to hold such a view is to think that there is, for each proper predicate of psychology, some one predicate of physics, such that satisfaction of the former is, with nomological necessity, a mere function of satisfaction of the latter. Other materialists have felt that an elaborately disjunctive answer could in principle be provided, by neurophysics, for the explanatory applicability of each proper predicate of psychology, taken individually. These materialists have felt, that is, that the explanatory usefulness of recognizing each individual satisfaction of each proper predicate of psychology *as* being that individual satisfaction of just predicate of psychology could, in principle, be explained by showing each such individual satisfaction to be identical with some individual satisfaction of some predicate of physics. This view too has, of course, been considered above. Our considerations suggest that neither of these commonly-envisioned answers can work. It is, however, at least formally possible to set out yet a third type of answer which materialists could, in consonance with their own basic approach, offer to the question of two-way explainability. That question formally could be answered, on the materialists' own formulation of it, simply by showing that the predicates of psychology as a class have explanatory applicability to that system of neurophysical events which is, on the materialist view, the behaviour of persons; it is not formally necessary that explanation be provided for the explanatory applicability of each psychological predicate individually. Explanation why predicates of psychology have, as a class, explanatory applicability to the behaviour of persons might, moreover, be undertaken by philosophy itself. Indeed one materialist philosopher has undertaken just such an explanation, namely Dennett in 'Intentional Systems'; the question has, however, been raised recently by Fodor as to whether Dennett's particular version is successful.[7]

It is natural that an answer to the question of two-way explainability drawn from the *Logic* should differ in its approach from all answers offered from the standpoint of materialism. For the fact that the predicates of psychology have explanatory and predictive applicability in the world is not, from the standpoint of the *Logic*, fundamentally problematic at all. The question of two-way explainability must therefore count, from the Hegelian standpoint, as a question about just that system of events to which the predicates of psychology do have explanatory and predictive applicability: what the question demands, on this reading, is an explanation why this very system of events also yields to explanation and prediction by use of the predicates of physics. Yet the same formal considerations hold true for answers from the Hegelian standpoint, as hold true for answers from the materialist standpoint. That is, it is sufficient that a Hegelian answer undertake to show why predicates of physics as a class have explanatory and predictive applicability to the system of events picked out by the predicates of psychology. Indeed it would seem that an answer even somewhat less specific than this would be sufficient to meet the demand raised, from the Hegelian standpoint, by the question of two-way explainability. For it would not seem to be crucial that a Hegelian answer explain why predicates of *physics*, in particular, should have explanatory applicability to the behaviour of persons; if it can be shown that the predicates of some natural science or other have such explanatory applicability, then the question would, it seems, adequately be answered. More precisely, the question is answered if it is shown that some family of predicates which provides for no references to intentions, purposes, beliefs, etc.—a family of predicates, that is, which does not provide for what recent discussion calls 'teleological explanation'—has explanatory and predictive force when applied to the system of events covered by psychology.

V. The answer on two-way explainability which emerges from the *Logic* is an answer of just this latter sort. This answer emerges from an analogy which can readily be drawn, and which Hegel himself partially indicates,[8] between positions which Hegel takes up on material objects, and positions which he takes up on rational, intentional agents.

The positions on material objects which are relevant here have, in effect, already been examined. Material objects, we have seen Hegel argue, are essentially the bearers of a certain role: they stand, essentially, as raw material for specific purposive endeavours, both practical and cognitive, by agents. As raw materials they elicit, they resist, and they yield to such purposive undertakings. This entails, then, that there necessarily are at least some material objects in the world which physically can be worked into conformity with specific practical ends. It also entails that purposive *work* must, precisely, be expended to bring about such conformity: the objects which will, under certain conditions, conform to specific practical ends, do not conform to ends either spontaneously or everlastingly. They essentially are such as to behave in accordance with blind and mechanical laws. Their behaviour may also be goal-serving or use-serving behaviour, in certain circumstances; but it is so only contingently.

Application of these familiar points to the question of two-way explainability requires that they be reformulated as points about the ways in which the behaviour of material objects can be explained and predicted. Dennett has pointed out that for some material objects, there are as many as three different systems by which their behaviour can be explained and predicted: the behaviour of Dennett's chess-playing computer can be explained, using 'intentional-stance' explanation, by referring to an intention, on the computer's part, to use the Dragon variation of the Sicilian Defense; the behaviour of an alarm clock can be explained, using 'design-stance' explanation, by saying that it rings now because it was set to go off now; and the behaviour of a clock without an alarm would be explained, by use of a 'physical-stance' explanation, if one said that it now produced a ringing sound because wheel A had come off its axle and was scraping against gear B.[9] What Hegel is saying, in the points repeated just above, can be reformulated as a claim about just these styles of explanation. For what Hegel maintains is, in effect, that for at least some material objects, there necessarily are some possible circumstances in which the behaviour of those objects yields to some design-stance explanation—some reference, that is, to a successfully implanted function or use—and that it also is a necessary truth, about these same material objects, that there are other possible circumstances in which their behaviour does not yield to design-stance explanation. In these other possible circumstances, only a physical-stance explanation will apply; only an explanation, that is, which draws on the blind and mechanical laws of the natural sciences.

Dennett's own position, it seems, is that for any material object, only the physical-stance explanation explains the events which *really* are occurring; and since Dennett evidently applies this position to persons as well as computers,[10] his ultimate position is at odds with Hegel's. Nevertheless the employment of Dennett's terminology is useful in formulating Hegel's points, since it permits us to notice one very important point of agreement between Hegel's position and Dennett's. Hegel sees, just as Dennett does, that physical-stance explanations apply not just in circumstances where a given object fails to serve some assigned use, but also in the very circumstances where that given object does serve its assigned use. For this reason, applicability of the physical-stance explanation necessarily outlasts applicability of the design-stance explanation; and there even is the suggestion, in certain of Hegel's remarks, that the predicates employed in design-stance explanations only pick out appearances or epiphenomena, and not features which really obtain. Thus Hegel writes, '. . . Even the executed End has the same radical rift or flaw as had the Means and the initial End. We have got . . . only a form extraneously impressed on a pre-existing material: and this form, by reason of the limited content of the End, is also a contingent characteristic. The End achieved consequently is only an object, which again becomes a Means or material for other Ends, and so on for ever' (*EL*, § 211). And note the employment of 'appears' in this similar passage:

> But the object that is supposed to contain the realized end, and to represent the objectivity of the end, is also perishable; it too fulfills its end not by a

tranquil existence in which it preserves itself, but only insofar as it is worn away. . . . A house, a clock may appear as ends in relation to the tools employed in their production; but the stones and beams, or wheels and axles, and so on, which constitute the activity of the end fulfil that end only through the pressure that they suffer, through the chemical processes with air, light, and water to which they are exposed and that deprive man of them by their friction and so forth.[11]

The views which Hegel takes on rational agents, to which these positions on material objects provide an important analogy, have not yet been explicitly considered in this monograph; they emerge quite readily, however, from views on rational agents which have been considered. Rational agents, we have seen Hegel hold, occupy a necessary place in any adequate embodiment of the Idea. For an adequate embodiment of the Idea must include not only agents which take on and pursue specific goals in open succession, thus taking on as their true end the second-order end of the pursuit, as such, of specific goals in general: it must also include agents which treat their true end as being thus general and openly variable; agents who also, as a consequence, treat their own agenthood as a case of an activity which equally is accomplishable in other lives as well. The only agents which match this description are, as we noted above, agents who perform conceptual and linguistic behaviour—rational agents, in the sense of our discussions.

Yet this same reasoning not only shows that rational agents are necessary for full embodiment of the Idea; it also shows that no *one* rational agent is, individually, necessary for that embodiment. What is needed, that is, is that there should be some careers of conceptual-linguistic behaviour. No need has been shown, and none exists, for there to be the conceptual-linguistic behaviours of just these particular agents, or of just those; as a contribution to embodiment of the Idea, any one career of conceptual-linguistic behaviour is replaceable, dispensable. And this point serves to explain certain other views which Hegel takes on rational agents, which have not yet been considered here; namely, that individual agents are *necessarily* susceptible to death, to disease, and to madness. For Hegel's general position is that the whole nature or essence of the individual rational agent—as of any other individual item—lies in the role which that agent plays in embodiment of the Idea.[12] If that role is by nature a dispensable role, that agent is by nature a dispensable agent.[13] The reasoning involved here can be set out as the following argument:

> Every individual career of conceptual-linguistic behaviour which occurs, occurs only contingently.

Every rational agent that exists possesses one, and only one, career of conceptual-linguistic behaviour.

∴ Concerning any rational agent that exists, the proposition *this agent exists & this agent possesses a career of conceptual-linguistic behaviour* is, at best, contingently true.

It therefore is possible—and necessarily possible—that any given rational agent should undergo disease, madness, or death.[14] But this is to say that there necessarily are phases, in the behaviour of which any individual agent is in principle capable, which are not explicable as rational, intentional behaviour. There necessarily are circumstances in which the behaviour of rational agents does not yield to explanation, and prediction, by use of the predicates of psychology.

We now are in a position to set Hegel's teachings on rational agents side by side with his teachings on material objects. Hegel maintains, concerning at least some material objects, that there necessarily are circumstances in which their behaviour is, or would be, explainable by reference to an implanted function; but that there also are, necessarily, circumstances in which the behaviour of these same objects is not, or would not be, thus explainable; and that, finally, susceptibility to such functional or design-stance explanation is no abiding feature of such material objects just because some other feature is. Material objects submit only under special circumstances to explanation by reference to function, just because they submit by nature to explanation of a different sort— namely, to explanation which, by referring to the physical features of material objects, subsumes material objects under physical laws. Now Hegel clearly maintains, concerning rational agents, that their behaviour genuinely is, at least in many circumstances, explainable and predictable by use of the predicates of psychology; Hegel does not, after all, regard the explanatory applicability of *these* predicates as problematic. At the same time, however, we have just seen Hegel to hold that there necessarily are circumstances in which the behaviour of these same agents does not, or would not, yield to explanation and prediction by use of the predicates of psychology. It would be natural for Hegel to hold, in this connection, a position analogous to the position which he takes on material objects. It would be natural for Hegel to hold, that is, that susceptibility to intentional explanation is no abiding feature of rational agents, just because some other feature is; that each individual agent yields only under special circumstances to explanation based on references to intentions, beliefs, and desires, just because each individual agent yields by nature to explanation based not on any such references, but on references to non-intentional, physical features. And this natural extension of Hegel's position on material objects would, in fact, constitute an answer to the question of two-way explainability. It would explain why the very beings whose behaviour yields, in large measure, to explanation and prediction by use of predicates of psychology, also were beings whose behaviour yields, in its entirety, to explanation and prediction by use of non-psychological predicates.

To say, however, that such a position on rational agents would be closely analogous to the position which Hegel takes up on material objects does not, by itself, establish that Hegel actually does take such a position; and neither does it show that such a position would be equally as defensible as that analogous position on material objects. These questions now require consideration in their own right. If we begin, then, with the former question, we find that comments which Hegel makes on rational agents both suggest that he does, and suggest that he does not, actually make the extension sketched here of his positions on material objects. Rational agents, we have seen Hegel to hold, necessarily are subject to behavioural episodes which do not yield to explanation as intentional agency, i.e. explanation by use of predicates depicting intentions, beliefs, desires, etc.; yet these same behavioural episodes do not, Hegel makes plain, simply lack specific explanations altogether. They do yield to specific explanations, and the explanations to which they yield are ones which subsume these episodes under the predicates of natural sciences. Thus far, then, Hegel does take up a position analogous to his position on material objects; for failures by objects to behave in a manner explained by an implanted function were themselves explained by 'the chemical process with air, light, and water', etc. (*SL*, p. 750). Yet the very passages in which Hegel asserts the explanatory applicability of natural sciences to episodes of human dysfunction are also passages in which Hegel suggests that natural sciences have explanatory applicability only to such dysfunctional episodes. Hegel fails, in other words, to extend his earlier insight, that explanatory applicability for the function-predicates employed in design-stance explanations, to a position that explanatory applicability for the predicates of natural science also can coexist with explanatory applicability for the predicates of psychology. The passages are these:

> The living body is always on the point of passing over into the chemical process; oxygen, hydrogen, salt, are always about to appear, but are always again sublated; and only at death or in disease is the chemical process able to prevail (*PN, Zusatz* to § 337).

> The living being stands face to face with an inorganic nature, to which it comports itself as a master and which it assimilates to itself. . . . But when the soul has fled from the body, the elementary powers of objectivity begin

their play. These powers are, as it were, continually on the spring, ready to begin their process in the organic body . . . (*EL, Zusatz* to § 219).

Should one say, then, that Hegel goes only part way in making his actual position on rational agents analogous to his positions on material objects? Reason for avoiding this judgement emerges as soon as one considers just what position on rational agents might be attributed to Hegel in place of the one sketched in the above analogy. Thus far we have seen Hegel hold that rational agents necessarily are subject to episodes of dysfunctional behaviour which satisfy predicates of natural science, and which moreover yield to explanation by natural science. It would seem, as a consequence, that Hegel must further hold that the episodes of functional behaviour, to which rational agents are also subject, themselves have descriptions under the predicates of natural science. If Hegel is to hold some view on rational agents other than the one sketched above, then, he must somehow make out the claim that the functional episodes of human behaviour do not, while the dysfunctional episodes of human behaviour do, yield to explanation by laws of natural science—and this despite the fact that either set of episodes is a set of episodes describable under the predicates of natural science. Now, support for just such a claim can in fact be found, namely in the position known as Vitalism. Vitalism explains that laws of natural science do not apply to healthy phases in the behaviour of an agent (or organism) just because, in such phases, a vital force is present in the agent, which influences the agent's physical behaviour; in dysfunctional episodes, such vital force is absent or weakened, and the laws of natural science therefore come to have explanatory and predictive force. Hegel himself makes reference to 'the soul', in the passage quoted second just above, and this reference may seem to suggest that vitalism is, precisely, the view which Hegel takes. But that reference occurs in a *Zusatz*, an oral comment addressed to Hegel's students. Hegel's formal discussion of soul, in *PM*, expresses an unqualified rejection of vitalism in any form; and it thereby suggests, indirectly, that the position on rational agents sketched above, as an extension of Hegel's position on material objects, may not, after all, be much at odds with thoughts Hegel actually had. Hegel starts that discussion by asserting, 'The soul is no separate immaterial entity' (*PM*, § 389). Yet neither is it a distinct material entity:

> But in modern times even the physicists have found matters grow thinner in their hands: . . . the *vital matter*, which may also be found enumerated among them, not merely lacks gravity, but even every other aspect of existence which might lead us to treat it as material (*PM*, § 389).

And Hegel comments, critically,

> When we go on to *reflection*, the opposition of soul and matter, of my
> subjective I and its bodily nature, becomes for us a fixed opposition, and
> the reciprocal relation of body and soul becomes an interaction of
> independent entities. The usual physiological and psychological treatment
> does not know how to overcome the fixity of this opposition. . . (*PM,
> Zusatz* to § 389).

There is therefore no straightforward answer as to whether Hegel
actually embraced the position on rational agents sketched in the above
analogy. That question is not, however, of central concern for our
present inquiry. The question which is of central concern for this inquiry
is whether Hegel provides—and not necessarily whether Hegel sees that
he provides—support for a position on rational agents which will furnish
an answer to the problem of two-way explainability. The position
sketched in the above analogy does furnish such an answer. And that
position is supported by Hegel's teaching that rational agents—being
nothing more than players of roles, individually dispensable, in the
embodiment of the Idea—are necessarily subject to episodes of
dysfunctional behaviour, *provided* that episodes of dysfunctional behaviour do yield to explanations of some sort, and *provided* that the
position taken by vitalists may be disregarded. No philosophical position
seriously entertained today provides support for doubts about the former
of these provisos. What remains is to show that the position taken by
vitalists may, indeed, legitimately be disregarded. The reason why it may
be disregarded, I contend, is that vitalism is internally inconsistent.

The inconsistency is connected with the very feature by which vitalism
secures its initial plausibility: namely with the concession, implicit in
vitalism, that physics (or other physical sciences) very well may, as is
commonly supposed, be such as to yield, in the long run, laws which
either are exceptionless or, at least, statistically true. For vitalism is
framed as a contention not about the accuracy, but rather about the
scope, of the physical sciences. It concedes that laws formulable by the
physical sciences may very well be highly accurate concerning their own
proper subject-matter; what it contends is that the subject-matter of
these laws does not include those episodes in the behaviour of agents and
organisms in which the 'vital force' is present and active. Vitalism does,
indeed, further maintain that if such behavioural episodes were subsumed under laws of physics, false predictions and misleading explanations would be generated. But the same might well occur if, for example,
creatures from some remote galaxy were subsumed under laws
formulated by biology or ethology: in either case the laws of a given

science would unjustly be faulted, on the vitalist view, for unreliability in some application which were, strictly speaking, irrelevant to that science. That this reasonable-sounding set of views is inconsistent, however, emerges as soon as one asks what predicates there are by which one may pick out the so-called vital force. Formally, two answers to this question are possible: one answer is that the vital force may be picked out by use of predicates of physics, and the other answer is that the vital force may be picked out only by use of predicates belonging to sciences other than physics, e.g. a vitalist biology. Yet actual vitalists have offered only the latter answer. For espousal of the former answer would force a choice, for vitalists, between two highly unattractive positions. If the vital force is picked out by some predicate of physics, then theorems about the vital force are, inevitably, entailed by the laws of physics; and vitalists would then have either to say that these theorems are false theorems, thus reneging on the concession that physics may be highly accurate, or else would have to retreat from the basic contention that activity of the vital force does not yield to explanation and prediction by physics.

Not surprisingly, then, vitalists in fact contend that the vital force cannot be picked out by use of any predicates of physics. But this position is in turn incompatible with the plausibility-gaining concession that physics can formulate highly accurate laws. For if physics cannot pick out the vital force, physics cannot qualify the assertions which it makes by any stipulation to the effect that this vital force must be absent or weakened. And physics inevitably will make assertions in connection with which such qualification is, on the vitalist view, required. For as vitalists themselves concede, every healthy state of a given agent or organism has some description—albeit an incomplete description— under the predicates of physics. But if so, then the laws of physics will inevitably generate theorems about what events must happen whenever each such description is satisfied; and these theorems will necessarily make no differentiation between satisfaction in the presence of the vital force, and satisfaction in its absence. And then if, as vitalism maintains, presence of the vital force renders predictions of physics inaccurate, physics will necessarily yield many predictions which commonly prove to be inaccurate. There is, moreover, yet a second respect in which physics must prove to be inaccurate, if vitalism in the present version is correct. Each dysfunctional state of a given organism, as vitalism also concedes, has some description under the predicates of physics. The laws of physics inevitably generate theorems, not just about what in fact happens when each such description is satisfied, but about what *must* happen when each such description is satisfied; the theorems entail counterfactuals. Now vitalists maintain that the vital force is capable of physically activating organisms independently of the laws of physics. This position would appear to entail that the vital force could—even if it never actually does—activate organisms which look, from their description under the predicates of physics, to be diseased or dead, so as to behave in the manner of healthy, living organisms. If so, however, the assertions entailed by physics about what must happen, when such standard descriptions of dysfunctional states are satisfied, will be false assertions.

Vitalism would therefore appear to be an incoherent view. But if it is an incoherent view, then Hegel's contentions about the susceptibility of each individual rational agent to disease, madness, and death entail that each individual rational agent has behaviour which, in its entirety, yields to explanation and prediction by use of non-pyschological predicates. Hegel's contentions therefore provide an answer to the question of two-way explainability.

Notes

PREFACE

1 Taylor (1972) and (1975), MacIntyre (1972b), and Bernstein (1977).

INTRODUCTION

1 *Logic,* §§ 204–212. From here on Wallace's translation of the Encyclopedia *Logic* will be referred to as *EL.*

2 In current discussions one sometimes finds the operation of final causes illustrated by reference, not to the action of an end by itself, but by reference to some desire for, or intention to produce, some end. Yet desires and intentions are particular states which exist prior to whatever realization of an end they may cause: they are therefore similar in kind to causes which contemporary discussion would mention as examples of *efficient* causes; whereas final causes were intended, by Aristotle, to be causes of a fundamentally different sort from efficient causes. (Aristotle himself would not have considered a state to be a suitable example of either a final, or an efficient, cause; but Aristotle's terminology is not simply modified, it is distorted, if no fundamental difference is retained between final and efficient causes.)

3 That is to say, there is an opposition between standard physical explanations—mechanistic explanations, as Hegel called them—and explanations based on finite teleology. See the *Science of Logic*, p. 374. From here on Miller's translation of this work will be referred to as *SL.*

4 *EL, Zusatz* to § 205. The illustration is repeated in Hegel's *Philosophy of Nature, Zusatz* to § 245 (from here on referred to as *PN*; see bibliography).

5 In the idea of infinite teleology, the concept of an End, which is used also in finite teleology, gets revised in a radical way. As so revised, the End amounts to what Hegel calls the Idea (*EL*, § 212). And in an early mention of the Idea, Hegel praises Aristotle for having (contrary to usual interpretations of Aristotle) made the Idea the central concept of his philosophy, and for having construed the Idea as an *energeia* (*EL, Zusatz* to § 142). Hegel also writes, in his actual introduction of the concept of infinite teleology—which he also refers to as inner (rather than outer) design—this remark:

'Aristotle's definition of life virtually implies inner design, and is thus far in advance of the notion of design in modern Teleology, which had in view finite and outward design only' (*EL*, § 204).

6 'The Means in its capacity of object stands, in this second premise, in direct relation to the other extreme of the syllogism, namely, the material or objectivity which is pre-supposed. This relation is the sphere of chemism and mechanism . . .' (*EL*, § 209).

7 Consider, for example, this sentence: 'All else is error, confusion, opinion, endeavor, caprice and transitoriness; the absolute Idea alone is *being,* imperishable *life, self-knowing truth,* and *is all truth*' (*SL*, p. 824).

8 'It is customary to treat Dialectic as an adventitious art. . . . But in its true and proper character, Dialectic is the very nature and essence of everything predicated by mere understanding. . . . the indwelling tendency outwards by which the one-sidedness and limitation of the predicates of understanding is seen in its true light, and shown to be the negation of them' (*EL*, § 81).

9 The phrase 'categories of surface description', like the phrase 'categories of explanation' below, is modelled after a similar phrase in J N Findlay's valuable Foreword to *EL* (see pp. xvii–xviii).

CHAPTER 1

1 *EL,* § 88, the paragraph Hegel numbers (1).

2 *EL,* § 88, the paragraph Hegel numbers (4); also the *Zusatz* to § 88.

3 Trendelenburg's well-known objection is that Hegel, by deriving the concept of Becoming here, smuggles in the concept of time. But Hegel indicates in § 88, in the paragraph he numbers (3), that the concept of Becoming is intended as a familiar *example* of the conceptual unity of Being and Nothing—a unity which, as paragraph (4) indicates, is founded on the conceptual opposition between Being and Nothing—to which the argument has directed our attention.

4 'Negation is no longer an abstract nothing, but, as a determinate being and somewhat, is only a form of such being—it is as Otherness' (*EL*, § 91).

5 *EL, Zusatz* to § 90. The point is repeated in a later passage: 'Property, besides, should not be confused with quality. No doubt, we also say, a thing has qualities. But the phraseology is a misplaced one: "having" hints at an independence, foreign to the "Somewhat" [= *Etwas*], which is still directly identical with its quality: whereas, though the thing indeed exists only as it has properties, it is not confined to this or that definite property, and can therefore lose it, without ceasing to be what it is' (*EL, Zusatz* to § 125).

6 *EL,* §§ 92–93. But see p. 5 below.

7 *EL,* § 93. See p. 5 below.

8 *EL,* § 95. Some commentators have considered Being-for-Self to be simply a separate concept from that of the determinate Something, rather than a universal of which each determinate Something is an instance. But Hegel indicates that Being-for-Self is a universal or, using the Platonic term, an 'idea':
'In Being-for-Self enters the category of Ideality' (*EL*, § 95). And that the determinate Somethings are all cases of this universal, is indicated in this passage: 'Thus essentially relative to another, somewhat [= *Etwas*, Something] is virtually an other against it: and since what is passed into is quite the same as what passes over, since both have one and the same attribute, viz. to be an other, it follows that something in its passage into other only joins with itself. . . . Thus Being . . . is now *Being-for-Self*' (*EL*, § 95). Indeed, that the

determinate Somethings *are* cases of Being-for-Self is the point of several comments which Hegel makes about Reality and Ideality, and about the finite and the infinite. Hegel says that Reality—of which the only instance so far is the determinate Something (*EL*, § 91)—must not be regarded as something distinct from Ideality; that is, that the real (the determinate Something) can be understood only by seeing it as a case of the ideal (the universal, Being-for-Self) (*EL, Zusatz* to § 91, § 95). Similarly, it would be a mistake, Hegel says, to credit the finite—of which the only example so far is the determinate Something (*EL*, § 92)—with a being of its own apart from the infinite; the infinite—of which Being-for-Self is the only formulation thus far—is rather the inner essence of the finite itself (*EL*, § 95).

9 'To be thus self-related in the passage, and in the other, is the genuine Infinity' (*EL*, § 95); '. . . but the determinateness is not in this case a finite determinateness —a somewhat in distinction from an other—but infinite, because it contains distinction absorbed and annulled in itself' (*EL, Zusatz* to § 96).

10 *EL, Zusatz* to § 106. The point is actually first made at the outset of Hegel's discussion of Quantity, in the first paragraph of the *Zusatz* to § 99.

CHAPTER 2

1 'The sphere of Essence thus turns out to be a still imperfect combination of immediacy and mediation. In it every term is expressly invested with the character of self-relatedness, while yet at the same time one is forced beyond it' (*EL*, § 114).

2 'These are products of the reflective understanding, which, while it assumes the differences to possess a footing of their own, and at the same time also expressly affirms their relativity, still combines the two statements, side by side, or one after the other, by an "Also", without bringing these thoughts into one, or unifying them into the notion' (*EL* § 114).

3 This example is modelled after one of Hegel's. Hegel mentions an 'explanation' of 'electrical phenomena' which points out that they are the work of 'electricity' (*EL, Zusatz* to § 121).

4 The regress through forces is narrated in *EL*, Zusatz (2) to § 136; the regress through ever smaller parts is mentioned in *EL*, § 136.

5 This is my reading of *EL*, §§ 141–142.

CHAPTER 3

1 In *SL*, not in *EL*.

2 Hegel considers, for example, the suggestion that the whole content of a given object consists in the role which it holds within ongoing chemical interaction, or else within the ongoing operation of a gravitational system; yet such roles as these, he promptly recognizes, cannot plausibly be said to make up the whole essence of the objects involved. 'In nature, for example, the several celestial bodies, which form our solar system, compose a kinetic system, and thereby show that they are related to one another. Motion, however, as the unity of time and space, is a connexion which is purely abstract and external. And it seems therefore as if these celestial bodies, which are thus externally connected with one another, would continue to be what they are, even apart from this reciprocal relation' (*EL, Zusatz* to § 200). And similarly chemical roles cannot be used to provide a re-conceptualization of objects as being, essentially, role-bearers within a project; chemical roles do not, as Hegel puts it, provide an adequate expression of the notion. 'The chemical process does not rise above a conditioned and finite process. The notion as notion is only the heart and core of the process, and does not in this stage come to an existence of its own' (*EL, Zusatz* to § 203).

3 To be precise, Hegel mentions a revised form of such social mechanism, in which a special social instinct is postulated to explain why agents fundamentally independent should nonetheless function as social beings. 'This is (2) *Mechanism with Affinity* (with bias, or "difference"), and may be illustrated by gravity, appetite, social instinct, etc.' (*EL*, § 196; see also § 198).

4 *PN*, §§ 325–326 and *Zusätze*.

5 'Accordingly, a chemical object is not comprehensible from itself alone, and the being of one is the being of the other' (*SL*, p. 728).

6 *EL*, § 205; *SL*, p. 735.

7 *EL*, § 211; *SL*, p. 750.

8 *EL*, §§ 221–222; see also *PN*, §§ 374–375 and *Zusätze*.

9 'The syllogism of the organism is, therefore, not the syllogism of *external teleology*, for it does not stop at directing its activity and form against the outer object but makes this very process, which is on the point of lapsing into a mechanical and chemical one, into an object' (*PN*, § 365, Remark).

10 See *PN*, § 361 and *Zusatz*.

11 See *PN*, §§ 367, 375 and 376; also *EL, Zusatz* to § 221, and § 222.

CHAPTER 4

1 Fodor (1975), pp. 9–26. See also Davidson (1970).

2 Fodor (1975), p. 15.

3 Ibid. pp. 15–16.

4 Fodor himself treats this objection as a plausible one; it is no serious threat to Fodor's functionalist approach to psychological states, since Fodor considers it likely that sensations are *not* psychological states, i.e. states falling in the domain of psychology. See Block and Fodor (1972). An ingenious defence of functionalism's claim to cover even sensations is given in Shoemaker (1975).

5 Fodor (1975), pp. 17–18.

6 See Block and Fodor (1972).

7 Dennett (1971), and Fodor (1979).

8 Both material objects and individual persons are, in Hegel's view, 'finite' things. Hegel states that this common 'finitude' entails parallel consequences for each of these two classes in *PN, Zusatz* to § 258. Again, both material objects and individual persons are 'individual beings', and this individuality is said to have parallel consequences in *EL*, § 213.

9 Dennett (1971), pp. 87–93.

10 Op. cit. pp. 96–97.

11 *SL,* p. 750. Consider also, in *EL,* § 209, this comment: 'This relation is the sphere of mechanism and chemism, which have now become servants of the Final Cause, where lies their truth and free notion.'

12 *EL,* § 213: 'Every individual being . . . which constitutes the finitude and the ruin of the individual.'

13 See *EL, Zusatz* to § 81: 'We say, for instance, that man is mortal . . . involves its own self-suppression.'

14 As to the susceptibility to madness, in particular, see the *Philosophy of Mind* (hereafter referred to as *PM*) § 408, and its *Zusatz* (especially p. 129). *PM* is also of interest in this connection as echoing, in the *Zusatz* to § 369, *EL* § 213: the series of stages in a person's life 'closes . . . with the triumph of the genus over individuality, with the abstract negation of the latter, with death' (p. 56).

Bibliography

CITED EDITIONS OF HEGEL

Hegel, G W F *SL, Science of Logic* translated by A V Miller (Allen and Unwin, 1969)
PN, Philosophy of Nature translated by A V Miller (Oxford University Press, 1970)
PM, Philosophy of Mind translated by William Wallace and A V Miller (Oxford University Press, 1971)
EL, Encyclopedia *Logic* translated by William Wallace (Oxford University Press, 1975)

OTHER WORKS

Bernstein, R J 1977, 'Why Hegel Now?' *Review of Metaphysics,* 31 (1977) 29-60
Block, N and Fodor, J A 1972, 'What Psychological States are not', *Philosophical Review,* 81 (1972) 159-181
Davidson, D 1970, 'Mental Events' in Foster, L, and Swanson, J, (eds), *Experience and Theory,* (University of Massachusetts Press)
Dennett, D C 1971, 'Intentional Systems' *Journal of Philosophy,* 68 (1971) 87-106
Fodor, J A 1975, *The Language of Thought* (Crowell)
1979, 'Three Cheers for Propositional Attitudes' in Cooper, W and Walker, E T (eds), *Sentence Recognition: Essays in Honour of Merrill Garrett* (Branford Press)
MacIntyre, A 1972a, *Hegel: a Collection of Critical Essays* (Doubleday)
1972b, 'Hegel on Faces and Skulls' in MacIntyre (1972a)
Shoemaker, S 1975, 'Functionalism and Qualia' *Philosophical Studies* 27 (1975) 291-315
Taylor, C 1972, 'The Opening Arguments of the *Phenomenology'* in MacIntyre (1972a)
1975, *Hegel* (Cambridge University Press)